Lynette Feder
Editor

Women and Domestic Violence: An Interdisciplinary Approach

Women and Domestic Violence: An Interdisciplinary Approach has been co-published simultaneously as *Women & Criminal Justice*, Volume 10, Number 2 1999.

Pre-publication
REVIEWS,
COMMENTARIES,
EVALUATIONS . . .

"This book has something that will be of interest for everyone. . . . learn different perspectives on domestic violence, both across and within your own discipline."

L. Kevin Hamberger, PhD
Professor
Department of Family
& Community Medicine
Medical College of Wisconsin

Women and Domestic Violence: An Interdisciplinary Approach

Women and Domestic Violence: An Interdisciplinary Approach has been co-published simultaneously as *Women & Criminal Justice*, Volume 10, Number 2 1999.

The *Women & Criminal Justice* Monographic "Separates"

Below is a list of "separates," which in serials librarianship means a special issue simultaneously published as a special journal issue or double-issue *and* as a "separate" hardbound monograph. (This is a format which we also call a "DocuSerial.")

"Separates" are published because specialized libraries or professionals may wish to purchase a specific thematic issue by itself in a format which can be separately cataloged and shelved, as opposed to purchasing the journal on an on-going basis. Faculty members may also more easily consider a "separate" for classroom adoption.

"Separates" are carefully classified separately with the major book jobbers so that the journal tie-in can be noted on new book order slips to avoid duplicate purchasing.

You may wish to visit Haworth's website at . . .

http://www.haworthpressinc.com

. . . to search our online catalog for complete tables of contents of these separates and related publications.

You may also call 1-800-HAWORTH (outside US/Canada: 607-722-5857), or Fax: 1-800-895-0582 (outside US/Canada: 607-771-0012), or e-mail at:

getinfo@haworthpressinc.com

The Criminalization of a Woman's Body, edited by Clarice Feinman, PhD (Vol. 3, No. 1/2, 1992). *"Addresses women's concerns worldwide about threats to their autonomy, privacy, and bodily integrity, focusing on the laws of various countries." (SciTech Book News)*

Women and Domestic Violence: An Interdisciplinary Approach, edited by Lynette Feder, PhD (Vol. 10, No. 2, 1999). *"An excellent overview of the criminal-justice response to domestic violence and is the best critical overview of the topic in print." (Evan Stark, PhD, MSW, Director, Domestic Violence Training Project, New Haven, CT)*

Women and Domestic Violence:
An Interdisciplinary Approach

Lynette Feder, PhD
Editor

Women and Domestic Violence: An Interdisciplinary Approach has been co-published simultaneously as *Women & Criminal Justice,* Volume 10, Number 2 1999.

The Haworth Press, Inc.
New York • London

Women and Domestic Violence: An Interdisciplinary Approach has been co-published simultaneously as *Women & Criminal Justice,* Volume 10, Number 2 1999.

The development, preparation, and publication of this work has been undertaken with great care. However, the publisher, employees, editors, and agents of The Haworth Press and all imprints of The Haworth Press, Inc., including The Haworth Medical Press® and Pharmaceutical Products Press®, are not responsible for any errors contained herein or for consequences that may ensue from use of materials or information contained in this work. Opinions expressed by the author(s) are not necessarily those of The Haworth Press, Inc.

The Haworth Press, Inc., 10 Alice Street, Binghamton, NY 13904-1580 USA

Cover design by Thomas J. Mayshock Jr.

Library of Congress Cataloging-in-Publication Data

Women and domestic violence: an interdisciplinary approach/Lynette Feder, editor.
    p. cm.
    Includes bibliographical references and index.
    ISBN 0-7890-0667-7 (alk. paper)
    1. Abused women–United States. 2. Abused wives–United States. 3. Family violence–United States. 4. Conjugal violence–United States. I. Feder, Lynette. II. Women & criminal justice.
HV6626.2.W64 1999
362.82'92'0973–dc21
                                    9911651
                                     CIP

INDEXING & ABSTRACTING

Contributions to this publication are selectively indexed or abstracted in print, electronic, online, or CD-ROM version(s) of the reference tools and information services listed below. This list is current as of the copyright date of this publication. See the end of this section for additional notes.

(continued)

99457

- *Social Planning/Policy & Development Abstracts (SOPODA)*
- *Social Work Abstracts*
- *Sociological Abstracts (SA)*
- *Studies on Women Abstracts*
- *Violence and Abuse Abstracts: A Review of Current Literature on Interpersonal Violence (VAA)*
- *Women Studies Abstracts*
- *Women's Studies Index* (indexed comprehensively)

Special Bibliographic Notes related to special journal issues (separates) and indexing/abstracting

- indexing/abstracting services in this list will also cover material in any "separate" that is co-published simultaneously with Haworth's special thematic journal issue or DocuSerial. Indexing/abstracting usually covers material at the article/chapter level.
- monographic co-editions are intended for either non-subscribers or libraries which intend to purchase a second copy for their circulating collections.
- monographic co-editions are reported to all jobbers/wholesalers/approval plans. The source journal is listed as the "series" to assist the prevention of duplicate purchasing in the same manner utilized for books-in-series.
- to facilitate user/access services all indexing/abstracting services are encouraged to utilize the co-indexing entry note indicated at the bottom of the first page of each article/chapter/contribution.
- this is intended to assist a library user of any reference tool (whether print, electronic, online, or CD-ROM) to locate the monographic version if the library has purchased this version but not a subscription to the source journal.
- individual articles/chapters in any Haworth publication are also available through the Haworth Document Delivery Service (HDDS).

Women and Domestic Violence: An Interdisciplinary Approach

CONTENTS

ABOUT THE EDITOR

Lynette Feder, PhD, received her doctorate from State University of New York at Albany, School of Criminal Justice in 1989. She is presently an Associate Professor in the Department of Criminal Justice at Florida Atlantic University. Dr. Feder has conducted research and published in areas of mentally ill offenders and their adjustment in the community, discrimination and the use of discretion in the criminal justice system, and police practices and domestic assault. She is presently conducting a federally funded classical experimental design to test the efficacy of court-mandated counseling for individuals convicted of misdemeanor domestic violence.

Acknowledgments

I want to take this opportunity to thank Dr. Lynette Feder of Florida Atlantic University for serving as the editor of this collection on domestic violence. Dr. Feder has completed this collection utilizing the same peer review process that is required of each volume. Each manuscript received is sent to three anonymous reviewers who have expertise in the subject matter of the manuscript. Therefore, I want to extend my appreciation to all the reviewers who advised Dr. Feder regarding publication.

Donna C. Hale
Editor

Domestic Violence:
An Interdisciplinary Approach

Lynette Feder

SUMMARY. This article serves as an introduction to this collection on domestic violence. The focus of the collection is on the use of an inter-disciplinary approach to the study of domestic violence. Only through such an approach will the various disciplines, as well as academics and professionals working in this area, come to understand the nature, causes, consequences and treatments for domestic violence. *[Article copies available for a fee from The Haworth Document Delivery Service: 1-800-342-9678. E-mail address: getinfo@haworthpressinc.com]*

INTRODUCTION

Historically, the "privilege" or beating one's wife has had social and legal approval in western civilization since ancient times. In the *Odyssey*, Homer makes reference to the authority men exercise over their wives and children without fear of the judgements of others (Taub, 1983). In the laws of marriage proclaimed by the Romans in 8th century BC, a married woman was obligated to obey her husband (Dobash & Dobash, 1978; Martin, 1987). He, in turn, had the moral and legal right to control and punish her should she misbehave (Stedman, 1917). In fact, this right to punish extended to the point of killing her where necessary (Hirschel & Hutchinson, 1992; Stedman, 1917). In this way, the man was given absolute power of life and death over his wife, as well as his children and slaves (Hilberman, 1980; Martin 1987). It

Lynette Feder, PhD, Associate Professor, Department of Criminal Justice, Florida Atlantic University, 777 West Glades Road, Boca Raton, FL 33431.

[Haworth co-indexing entry note]: "Domestic Violence: An Interdisciplinary Approach." Feder, Lynette. Co-published simultaneously in *Women & Criminal Justice* (The Haworth Press, Inc.) Vol. 10, No. 2, 1999, pp. 1-7; and: *Women and Domestic Violence: An Interdisciplinary Approach* (ed: Lynette Feder) The Haworth Press, Inc., 1999, pp. 1-7. Single or multiple copies of this article are available for a fee from The Haworth Document Delivery Service [1-800-342-9678, 9:00 a.m. - 5:00 p.m. (EST). E-mail address: getinfo@haworthpressinc.com].

1

is interesting to note that the word "family" comes from the Latin word "familia" which in Roman culture connoted the totality of slaves belonging to a man (Hilberman, 1980; Martin, 1987).

With the ascendancy of the Church, the husband's rule over his wife was explicitly written into the laws of the church (Davidson, 1977; Dobash & Dobash, 1978). Contained in the *Decretum*, the first enduring systematization of church law, was the Church's view of the proper role of a wife. "Adam was beguiled by Eve, not she by him. It is right that he whom woman led into wrongdoing should have her under his direction, so that he may not fail a second time through female levity" (Davidson, 1977).

Just as this view of the wife had been woven into church ideology, it now was embedded in common law traditions. However, while male authority did not include the power of life and death, physical chastisement was accepted and expected in England (Hirschel & Hutchinson, 1992). According to the British doctrine of coverture, upon being married, a husband and wife became a single legal entity in the eyes of the law. Not surprisingly, that entity was the husband's as the wife thereafter lost all legal standing (Dobash & Dobash, 1978; Eisenberg & Micklow, 1977). Quite logically this led to the view that the husband had the responsibility to control his wife. As noted by Blackstone in 1763, "For, as he is to answer for her misbehaviors, the law thought it reasonable to entrust him with the power of restricting her by chastisement" (Davidson, 1977).

The English colonists coming to America brought these attitudes with them. Domestic violence existed in the New World just as it had in England (Martin, 1987). Indifference or outright approval of the right to chastise was maintained well into the 1800s (Hirschel & Hutchinson, 1992). Eventually, though, state courts rejected the right of a husband to physically punish his wife (Eisenberg & Micklow, 1977; Greenblat, 1985). However, even as the courts ruled wifebeating illegal, they added that moderate chastisement (meaning assaults not leaving permanent injury) should be viewed as a private matter (Taub, 1983) best left outside the purview of the law [*State v. Oliver*, 70 N.C. 60, 61-62, 1873].

Even as the criminal justice system and others showed disinterest in the subject of domestic violence, the magnitude of the problem spoke clearly to this issue warranting serious attention. Since this behavior is almost always done behind closed doors, bringing disgrace to both victim and offender, an actual count of the incidence and prevalence of domestic violence is impossible to determine. In fact, based on his thorough review of the research on measuring and reporting domestic violence, Dutton estimates that more than 92% of all incidences of domestic violence in North America remain private (Dutton, 1988).

With that in mind, government figures based on domestic violent incidents reported to the police indicate that 3,000 women die yearly (Friedman & Shulman, 1990), and among all female victims of murders, more than one-quarter are believed to have been slain by their husbands or boyfriends (Harlow, 1991). However, we know that these numbers greatly undercount the true amount of spousal violence since they rely on only the most violent events that are more likely to come to the police's attention (Stanko, 1988).

One well-regarded study indicated that victim interview surveys provided higher numbers of domestic violent incidents than that reported by the police (Hirschel, Hutchinson & Dean, 1992). But victim interviews have also been shown to undercount the true incidence of violence committed at the hands of intimates (San Jose Methods Test, 1972). The problem with victim interview surveys is that victims may be unwilling to report these victimizations because of shame or fear of reprisal. Additionally, the government's annual victimization survey–the National Crime Victimization Survey (NCVS)–is described to respondents as a *crime* survey. Research indicates that this may lead to undercounting since women may not identify themselves as victims of crime when assaulted by their husbands and boyfriends (Dutton, 1987; Dutton, 1988; Smith, 1984). With these caveats in mind, NCVS indicates that more than 572,000 women experience one or more violent victimizations at the hand of an intimate each year (Bachman, 1994).

Another widely used instrument, the Straus Conflict Tactics Scale (CTS), is based on victim and offender self-reports. However, unlike the NCVS, the CTS does not describe itself as a *crime* survey. Using this scale, the 1985 National Family Violence Survey estimated that there were 8.7 million domestic assault victims yearly. In other words, approximately 16% of cohabiting couples in the United States were involved in one or more incidents of domestic violence yearly (Straus, 1991). Beyond the large numbers, the severity of these incidents also indicates cause for concern. One-third of domestic violence incidents reported in NCVS would be classified as felonies (Friedman & Shulman, 1990; Langan & Innes, 1986). Women who are victimized by an intimate are twice as likely to be injured as those victimized by strangers (Bachman, 1994; Langan & Innes, 1986).

Gelles and Straus (1985) have noted:

> With the exception of the police and the military, the family is perhaps the most violent social group, and the home the most violent social setting, in our society. . . . Nearly one out of every four murder victims in the United States is a family member. . . . Although increased public attention to the problem of family violence would suggest that there has been a rapid increase in the level of family violence, most historical evidence suggests that the family has always been one of society's more violent institutions. But despite the family's long history as a violent

social setting, for many years the issue of violence in the home was subjected to "selective inattention." (Gelles & Straus, 1985:88)

THE NEED FOR AN INTERDISCIPLINARY APPROACH

There is no doubt that, after years of selective inattention, the problem of domestic violence deserves to be the focus of academics and professionals. And, in fact, it is now receiving wide attention from many different circles. At present, it truly cannot be viewed as the domain of any one discipline. It is easily a study which is "transdisciplinary"–that is, its themes transcend or cross over several disciplines (Davis, 1995).

But dialogues between and among disciplines are occurring with greater frequency. And in this manner we are happily becoming more of an "interdisciplinary" study with that term signifying a higher level of integration among the various disciplines studying this problem. The family violence researchers out of University of New Hampshire will hold their 6th Annual International Family Violence Conference this summer. A quick perusal of last year's participant directory clearly indicates the many different disciplines that were represented at the conference. And last year, family violence became the subject of a Request for Application sponsored jointly by agencies as disparate as Center for Disease Control, National Center on Child Abuse and Neglect, National Institute of Justice, and several institutes within the National Institute of Health including the National Institute of Aging, National Institute of Alcohol Abuse and Alcoholism, National Institute of Drug Abuse, National Institute of Mental Health and the National Institute of Nursing Research.

The most wonderful aspect about being an editor is that one has the opportunity to put forward a subject the way they wish it to be presented. For me the choice was simple–to continue to build upon this dialogue occurring between disciplines on the topic of domestic violence. As such, this collection presents readings from a historian, lawyer, criminologist, and psychologist. The requirements for submission were simple. Each author, in addition to providing a cursory overview of the relevant literature in their area, was asked to approach the topic from the particular perspective of their discipline. The manuscript submissions were then subject to blind review from three experts in each of the authors' disciplines, in addition to separate review by the guest editor. Since the readings are from different disciplines, they may at first seem uneven were one to read this issue from front to back covers. As editor I must confess that I do not necessarily view this as a disadvantage. Instead, this is seen as a direct result of having each author address the study in the voice of his or her own discipline.

In "Revisiting the Rule of Thumb: An Overview of The History of Wife

Abuse," Susan A. Lentz provides a historical analysis on domestic violence in America, tracing its roots solidly in the western tradition. She sees this issue surfacing then fading then resurfacing at different periods of time. However, even when domestic violence receives attention, the one constant is the system's failure to provide enough resources for beaten wives.

There are more than a few articles detailing the remedies presently available to victims of domestic violence through the criminal law (see Buzawa & Buzawa, 1985; Lerman, 1982; Lerman, Livingston & Jackson, 1983). However, Catherine F. Klein and Leslye E. Orloff provide a fuller understanding on the relief available to victims through civil protection orders in their article entitled "Protecting Battered Women: Latest Trends in Civil Legal Relief." They then proceed to identify emerging trends in civil protection order law.

In the article, "Police Handling of Domestic Violence Calls: An Overview and Further Investigation," I provide a literature review of the research on police likelihood to arrest when responding to domestic assault calls, along with the correlates related to this decision. I then go on to provide a comparison of two methods for assessing police handling of these calls–police self-report surveys and police case record analysis.

Finally, in their article entitled, "Does Batterer Treatment Reduce Violence? A Synthesis of the Literature," Robert C. Davis and Bruce G. Taylor provide an extensive review of the research literature on the efficacy of court-mandated counseling for misdemeanor domestic violence offenders. They provide a thoughtful critique of the research done to date testing the impact of court-mandated counseling on this particular offender population. They conclude by providing results from their own rigorous study using a classical experimental design.

The articles that follow, then, provide an assortment of readings from various disciplines on different aspects of domestic violence. I am indebted to the fine authors I worked with to make this edition a reality. And I am grateful for the large amounts of time and expertise that our twelve reviewers so willingly shared to make each article the best it could be. Finally, special thanks to Dr. Donna Hale for her gentle guidance and support through what proved to be a rather steep learning curve.

BIBLIOGRAPHY

Bachman, Ronet. (1994). *Violence Against Women*. Washington, DC: US Department of Justice NCJ-145325.

Buzawa, Eve & Buzawa, Carl. (1985). Legislative trends in the criminal justice response to domestic violence. In A Lincoln & M. Straus (Eds.), *Crime in the family* (pp. 134-147). Springfield, IL: Charles C. Thomas.

Davidson, Terry. (1977). Wifebeating: A recurring phenomenon throughout history.

In M. Roy (Ed.), *Battered women: A psychosociolgical study of domestic violence* (pp. 2-23). New York: Van Nostrand Reinhold.

Davis, James. (1995). *Interdisciplinary Courses and Team Teaching.* New York: Onyx Press.

Dobash, R. Emerson & Dobash, Russell. (1978). Wives: The "appropriate" victims of marital violence. *Victimology: An International Journal, 2*(3-4), 426-442.

Dutton, Donald. (1987). The criminal justice response to wife assault. *Law and Human Behavior, 11*(3), 189-206.

Dutton, Donald. (1988). Research advances in the study of wife assault: Etiology and prevention. *Law and Mental Health, 4,* 161-220.

Eisenberg, Sue & Micklow, Patricia. (1977). The assaulted wife: "Catch 22" revisited. *Women's Rights Law Reporter, 3,* pp. 138-164.

Friedman, Lucy & Shulman, Minna. (1990). Domestic violence: The criminal justice response. In A. Lurigio, W. Skogan, & R. Davis (Eds.), *Victims of crime: Problems, policies, and programs* (pp. 87-103). Newbury Park, CA: Sage Publications.

Gelles, Richard & Straus, Murray. (1985). Violence in the American family. In A. Lincoln & M. Straus (Eds.), *Crime in the family* (pp. 88-110). Springfield, IL: Charles C. Thomas.

Greenblat, Cathy. (1985). "Don't hit your wife. . . unless. . .": Preliminary findings on normative support for the use of physical force by husbands. *Victimology: An International Journal, 10*(1-4), pp. 221-241.

Harlow, Caroline Wolf. (1991). *Female victims of violent crime.* Washington, DC: US Department of Justice, Bureau of Justice Statistics.

Hilberman, Elaine. (1980). Overview: The "wife-beater's wife" reconsidered. *American Journal of Psychiatry, 137*(11), pp. 1336-1347.

Hirschel, J. David & Hutchinson, Ira. (1992). Female spouse abuse and the police response: The Charlotte, North Carolina Experiment. *Journal of Criminal Law and Criminology, 83*(1), pp. 73-119.

Hirschel, J. David, Hutchison, Ira, & Dean, Charles. (1992). The failure of arrest to deter spouse abuse. *Journal of Research in Crime and Delinquency, 29*(1), pp. 7-33.

Langan, Patrick, & Innes, Christopher. (1986). *Preventing domestic violence against women.* Washington, D.C.: U.S. Department of Justice, National Institute of Justice.

Lerman, Lisa. (1982). Expansion of arrest power: A key to effective intervention. *Vermont Law Review, 7,* pp. 59-70.

Lerman, Lisa, Livingston, Franci & Jackson, Vicky. (1983). State legislation on domestic violence. *Response to Violence in the Family and Sexual Assault, 6*(5), pp. 1-27.

Martin, Del. (1987). The historical roots of domestic violence. In D.J. Sonkin (Ed.), *Domestic Violence on Trial* (pp. 3-20). New York, NY: Springer Publishing Company.

San Jose Methods Test of Known Crime Victims. (1972). *Statistics Technical Report No. 1.* Washington, D.C.: National Institute of Law Enforcement and Criminal Justice Statistics Division, Law Enforcement Assistance Administration.

Smith, Michael. (1994). Enhancing the quality of survey data on violence against women: A feminist approach. *Gender & Society, 8,* pp. 109-127.

Stanko, Elizabeth. (1988). Hidden violence against women. In M. Maguire & J. Pointing (Eds.), *Victims of crime* (pp. 40-46). Philadelphia, PA: Open University Press.

Stedman, Beirne. (1917). Right of husband to chastise wife. *Virginia Law Reporter, 3*(4), pp. 241-248.

Straus, Murray. (1991). Conceptualization and measurement of battering: Implications for public policy. In M. Steinman (Ed.), *Woman Battering: Policy Responses* (pp. 19-47). Cincinnati, Ohio: Anderson Publishing.

Taub, Nadine. (1983). Adult domestic violence: The law's response. *Victimology: An International Journal, 8*(1-2), pp. 152-171.

Revisiting the Rule of Thumb:
An Overview of the History
of Wife Abuse

Susan A. Lentz

SUMMARY. This writing provides a brief overview of the history of wife abuse and its roots in traditions of patriarchy. Historically the wife was without independent legal status and generally outside the protection of the law. This was largely true in regard to wife abuse. Over the centuries a variety of interventions attempted to alleviate the harsher aspects of such abuse, with limited success. Yet, gradual change did occur in attitudes, law, and patriarchy. This history is itself a prologue to the elimination of domestic violence in today's society. *[Article copies available for a fee from The Haworth Document Delivery Service: 1-800-342-9678. E-mail address: getinfo@haworthpressinc.com]*

In the covenant of marriage, she is compelled to promise obedience to her husband, he becoming, to all intents and purposes, her master–the law giving him power to deprive her of liberty, and to administer chastisement.

–Declaration of Sentiments, 1848

INTRODUCTION

These words echo across the centuries, women speaking about wife abuse, politely called chastisement. Yet, these words were only part of a larger

---

Susan A. Lentz, Assistant Professor, Criminal Justice, University of Nevado, Reno. She received her Ph.D. in history from the University of Wisconsin-Madison and her J.D. from the University of Denver.

[Haworth co-indexing entry note]: "Revisiting the Rule of Thumb: An Overview of the History of Wife Abuse." Lentz, Susan A. Co-published simultaneously in *Women & Criminal Justice* (The Haworth Press, Inc.) Vol. 10, No. 2, 1999, pp. 9-27; and: *Women and Domestic Violence: An Interdisciplinary Approach* (ed: Lynette Feder) The Haworth Press, Inc., 1999, pp. 9-27. Single or multiple copies of this article are available for a fee from The Haworth Document Delivery Service [1-800-342-9678, 9:00 a.m. - 5:00 p.m. (EST). E-mail address: getinfo@haworthpressinc.com].

documentation of the abuses of husbands toward their wives itemized at the Seneca Falls Convention in 1848. For a long time they were overshadowed by issues of women's economic and political autonomy.

The history of spousal abuse in the United States itself also remains to a degree in the shadows. This is where spousal battery has so long remained, unspoken behind closed doors. While the Seneca Falls Declaration illuminates this history, much remains obscure. Today, what is most remembered about wife abuse is the so-called rule of thumb, the doctrine that permitted American husbands to correct their wives with rods no bigger than their thumb. Yet, the rule itself, its origins and impact remain somewhat enigmatic. Sources on spousal abuse include treatises on the law, theological tracts, expressions of popular culture, court records, and philosophical or political tracts. Most often, they address wife abuse tangentially, even offhandedly. While much research remains to be done, during recent decades, historians and other scholars have collected a valuable record of information spanning the centuries that begin to pierce the darkness behind those closed doors.

The purpose of this writing is to outline the contours of the history of wife abuse. In such a brief space, not all dimensions of its history nor the breadth of its scholarship can be presented. Nevertheless, within its outline, common themes become threads to be woven into a yet incomplete tapestry. Themes of the rule of husbands and the legitimacy of chastisement, wife blaming, and the limits of correction within the community, law and popular culture recur. The tapestry reveals both continuity and change. Within such evolution, there have been times of government intervention and legal change followed by retrenchment and lost opportunities. Greater knowledge about recent history tends to emphasize change. Yet, the roots of wife abuse in American history are buried deep in the past.

THE ROOTS OF CHASTISEMENT

Traditions subordinating women have a long history rooted in patriarchy—the institutional rule of men. Women were seen in virtually all societies to be naturally inferior both physically and intellectually. In ancient western societies, women, whether slave, concubine or wife, were under the authority of men. In law, they were treated as property (Anderson and Zinsser, Vol. I, 1989). As men ruled in government and society, so husbands ruled in the home.

The Rule of Men and Husbands

Christianity inherited earlier traditions of subordination (Anderson and Zinsser, 1989, Vol. I; Davidson, 1977). During the twelfth century, Gratian in the *Decretum*, the first systematic document of church law, reinforced the rule of husbands by emphasizing that women were not made in the image of God. Since woman had brought about the fall of man, it was "right that he whom woman led into wrongdoing would have her under his direction, so that he may not fail a second time through female levity" (cited in Davidson, 1977: 11-12). The companionate marriage of the Protestant Reformation did little to alter the "ideal" family relationship. As Martin Luther wrote in the sixteenth century, "The rule remains with the husband, and the wife is compelled to obey him" (cited in Anderson and Zinsser, Vol. I: 259).

Whatever the justification for the rule of husbands, from it flowed certain rights and responsibilities. In law, the identity of the wife merged with the husband. (For a detailed discussion of women in early Western societies, see Anderson and Zinsser, 1989, Vol. I; for a detailed discussion of women in the Old Testament, see Davidson, 1977.) In England, under feudal law a wife became a "femme covert," under the protection and cover of her husband (Anderson and Zinsser, Vol. 1: 338). Under the doctrine of coverture, the husband became legally responsible for his wife's actions. She was restricted in her ability to contract, to own and manage real property, and to sue or be sued. Although a detailed discussion of the history of coverture is beyond the scope of this writing, modern scholars confirm the significance of the doctrine in the shaping of married women's public and private lives. Wives remained economically as well as legally dependent on their husbands. (For discussions of coverture, see, for example, Frey and Morton, 1986; Salmon, 1986.) The importance of such dependence in regard to wife abuse would not come to the forefront of society's consciousness until the nineteenth century.

As master, the husband was responsible for order in the home and for the spiritual and moral well being of the family. In regard to the rule of husbands, St. Augustine (1977: 78) wrote in the fifth century that for "domestic peace" it was necessary that "they who care for the rest rule–the husband the wife, the parents the children, the masters the servants; and they who are cared for obey–the women their husbands, the children their parents, the servants their masters." In this Christian family and household, rule was not for a love of power but from a "sense of duty" (79). According to Augustine (79), "if any member of the family interrupts the domestic peace by disobedience, he is corrected either by word or blow, or some kind of just and legitimate punishment, such as society permits. . . ." In the centuries that followed, there emerges a theme of just chastisement, and a notion of reasonableness.

In general, any perceived threat to a husband's authority warranted correction. The reasonableness of a particular form of chastisement was tied to its justification, to what the wife had done to deserve the scolding or beating (Anderson and Zinsser, Vol. 1, 1988; Okun, 1986). The appropriateness of physical chastisement or beating remained largely unchallenged until the decades following the Protestant Reformation. In the later decades of the sixteenth century, a public debate emerged in England regarding chastisement in general, and beating in particular (Doggett, 1992; Fletcher, 1995; Amussen, 1994). William Gouge in his *Domestical Duties* declared that physical chastisement was never appropriate; others suggested that it might be appropriate in cases of extreme provocation (Doggett, 1992; Ingram, 1987). The courts also began to question wife beating as a form of chastisement (Doggett, 1992). This debate persisted throughout much of the 1600s. Continued legal confusion and ambivalence in regard to chastisement can perhaps be attributed in part to the persistence of wife blaming, of accepting provocation as a defense. The condemnation of physical beating, however, suggests that a shift in attitudes, or values, had begun during the seventeenth century, at least in a segment of English society.

Although no new consensus emerged, Amussen (1994) concludes that rules existed. Correction was supposed to be in response to a "particular fault, not the result of generalized anger" (Amussen, 1994: 82). Only moderate correction was permitted. If a husband behaved unreasonably, the community would intervene. This notion of reasonableness also reflected a level of accepted and acceptable violence in society.

Popular Culture and Public Violence

According to Amussen (1994: 84), domestic violence has always been "rooted in particular sets of community values." Anderson and Zinsser (1988) and Davis (1971) assert that women had long been particular targets of violence. Quasi-legitimate forms of violence included not only public executions, whippings and mutilation, but also spousal correction (Amussen, 1994; also Beattie, 1986). Unlike later distinctions emphasizing the private nature of the family, Amussen (1994) notes that the family had long had a public nature and been viewed as a "small state." As a public concern, neighbors and other members of the community did at times intervene to limit family violence. Clark (1992) and Hunt (1995) add, however, that formal intervention of the courts only occurred in cases of extreme violence.

The public nature of such violence also found expression in popular culture. Mocking husbands who did not control their wives was a recurring theme from Medieval community plays, or charivari, to effigies, popular ballads and rhymes of the eighteenth century (Davidson, 1977; Fletcher, 1995). According to Ingram (1987) the ridicule of the cuckold or battered husband warned against subverting the proper order of the family. At the same time, it tended to stigmatize extreme violations of the patriarchal ideal. Debate remains regarding how much attitudes were changing across class boundaries. Fletcher (1995) suggests that wife beating came to be viewed as a mark of the lower classes, at least by the upper classes who increasingly disdained such violence. In turn, what happened in upper class families became "veiled in silence" (201).

Acknowledgment of spousal abuse and the public debate that surrounded it in England occurred at the same time that colonists were migrating to America. The English debate was largely prompted by religious, social, and political upheaval that began with the Protestant Reformation and continued in the civil wars of the seventeenth century. The colonial experience itself to a significant degree grew out of this ferment. Thus, common threads appear.

CHASTISEMENT IN COLONIAL AMERICA

Colonial isolation left room for significant variation in regard to many aspects of married life. Condemnation of wife beating which had stimulated public debate in England also appeared in those American colonies under Puritan influence. In the New England colonies, marriage was to a degree redefined. Although New England colonists did not view wives as equal to their husbands civilly, they did recognize that women were the spiritual equals of men. In this, women were no longer bound to the story of Eve and wives were elevated in the family, yet still subordinate. The man who relied on the patriarchal ideal of the husband as ruler and the wife as servant to justify physical chastisement found himself at the margin of his community (Harris, 1978). According to Ulrich (1992: 108), the Protestant ideal of marriage was the notion of "consort," where "Reciprocal affection transformed commands (of the husband) into helpfulness and obedience (of the wife) into support. . . . " Marital disharmony was unlikely to occur if a husband were kind, if a wife were obedient and modest. (See also Benson, 1935; Riley, 1991; Bailey, 1989.) When either brought discord, the community could, and would, respond to protect the social order which was essential in the new world.

In the New England colonies the first remedy for marital conflict was "individual reformation and self-control" (Ulrich, 1992: 110). Family and church members often attempted to mediate marital disputes. As Pleck (1987:18) notes, "meddling" was a "positive virtue" in Puritan society. Churches could also censure their members for marital violence (Speth and Hirsch, 1983). In addition, criminal prosecutions were recognized. Unlike England, where prosecutions for wife assault were apparently only recognized by the courts in the later decades of the seventeenth century (Doggett, 1992; Clark, 1992), the New England colonies of Massachusetts Bay and Plymouth enacted legislation making wife beating criminal (Treckel, 1996). Community members were bound by law to report such abuse. According to Pleck (1987), complaints under such laws, however, declined during the eighteenth century as the Puritan sense of community morality eroded.

Although the severity of the chastisement was a factor in securing community intervention, the character and reputation of the victim were also important. Ulrich (1982) concludes that the submissive wife was more likely to be protected by the authorities. As Pleck notes (1987), Puritans only sided with the blameless. Where the wife was seen to provoke the beating, the husband was more likely to be treated leniently (Ulrich, 1982), and unruly wives who beat their husbands faced the harshest condemnation (Treckel, 1996). According to Treckel (1996: 147), recantations were common and "preserving the family took precedence over punishing the abuser." (See also Riley, 1991.)

Divorce and Legal Separation

While the New England colonists sought to preserve family harmony, they also recognized that extreme marital discord could threaten the fabric of the society. Unlike England, they viewed marriage as a civil contract, or covenant, and provided for absolute divorce through legislative or court action (Salmon, 1986; Frey and Morton, 1986; Woloch, 1992). Nevertheless, the grounds for absolute divorce remained limited. Near the end of the seventeenth century some New England leaders called for the liberalization of divorce laws because marital disharmony led to social disorder. The ending of a marriage could itself protect the institution of marriage and the family (Riley, 1991). Although cruelty came to be recognized as a ground for divorce, it generally had to be coupled with other grounds such as desertion and evidentiary standards were often high (see, for example, the case of Abigail Abbott Bailey in the late eighteenth century; Bailey, 1989).

In all colonies, legal separation was the more common form of marital dissolution. It was also recognized in England. Legal separation was essentially divorce from bed and board: it did not permit remarriage and, in theory, husbands remained obligated to support their wives. (See, for example, the letter of June 8, 1681 to the Attorney General of Maryland, Frey and Morton, 1986:95.) Cruelty had been acknowledged as grounds for such separation in England as early as the Middle Ages (Leyser, 1995). In the colonies, extreme cruelty was widely recognized (Riley, 1991), but to obtain a separation, the successful petitioner generally had to show that she was a "good wife" (Treckel, 1996). The most common grounds for dissolution remained adultery and desertion.

Legal Status and Equity

In some colonies, the law of equity afforded wives another option. While equity or chancery courts were not widely adopted in the colonies, equity law was brought to America. Equity addresses fairness in providing remedies not available in other claims or courts. Under certain circumstances, contracts between husbands and wives, even contracts of separation became enforceable (Salmon, 1986). Both antenuptial and postnuptial agreements existed (Woloch, 1992; in regard to the English practice, see Doggett, 1992). In reality, legal options remained very limited for women during the colonial period. Besides being very public, they were often not financially accessible. According to Woloch (1992), it was far more common for marriages "to end" not by legal action but by simple abandonment, as was also true in England.

Although seeds of change appeared in the colonies, the law of coverture still largely upheld patriarchy. In some colonies, however, wives began to have certain limited rights in regard to the ownership and management of property. Under certain circumstances, they were permitted to act as independent traders or entrepreneurs (Salmon, 1986; Harris, 1978). These new opportunities were not only limited but also a mixed blessing: on the one hand, greater property rights enhanced the social status of women. On the other, they created a new source of marital tension. For this reason, the Puritan colonies of New England continued to bar women from owning separate property, but they did permit certain types of contracts that did not challenge the husband's rule (Treckel, 1996). The ability of a wife to make her own choices could also readily be perceived by her husband as insubordination. According to Treckel (1996), to prevent the coercion of husbands in regard to conveyances, some colonies enacted laws requiring that wives be privately examined about the sale or mortgaging of property. (See also, Frey and Morton; 1986; Salmon, 1986.) As the eighteenth century progressed, Frey and Morton (1986) suggest that the private examination became less formal, and perhaps honored in the ideal rather than the reality.

THE NEW NATION

As the new nation emerged, Eliza Wilkinson, after seeing a husband beat his wife in 1781, wrote a poem that expressed the hopes and fears of young women regarding the state of marriage, and their futures:

Poor Wives are made to Honour and obey.
Must yield unto a husband's lordly sway.
Whether you live in Peace, or horrid strife,
You must stay with him, aye, and that for life.
If he proves kind, then happy you will be,
If otherways–O! dreadful misery!. . . .
(Frey and Morton, 1986: 207-208)

In Europe and America, there was great political ferment, philosophical debate, and scientific discovery. In the seventeenth century, philosophers such as Thomas Hobbes and John Locke had rejected the notion of natural subordination and emphasized the importance of a social contract, contributing to political change. In reality, they did not reject the subordination of women and traditional notions of family. Although such attacks on hierarchy eventually affected the lives of married women, there was much resistance. The marriage contract was not truly like the political contract, based on free consent among equals, among men. According to Clark (1992), a married woman entered into a sexual contract where she consented to obey her husband in return for protection. She consented to her own subordination. These contradictions contributed to ambiguity in the law regarding chastisement (Clark, 1992).

Middle Class Challenges to Chastisement

The greater refinement of "the ideology of separate spheres" (Clark, 1992: 191), of public and private worlds, at this time also permitted the social contract to remain a paradox. While revolutions for men stirred across the oceans, women remained in the private domain of the home. According to Gordon (1988) and Riley (1991), separate spheres alleviated some of the tension in middle class marriages. Husbands and wives ruled in their own domains. Sexual hierarchy began to shatter (Griswold, 1982). Greater expectations could, however, also increase tensions (Riley, 1991). As noted above, among the middle and upper classes of both England and America, wife beating began to be condemned in the seventeenth century. By the nineteenth century, it was generally no longer acceptable as a form of chastisement (Gordon, 1988; Clark, 1992). Yet, this does not mean that it did not exist among those classes (see, e.g., Cobbe, 1994; also Fletcher, 1995). Tomes (1978) concludes that, in reality, there was no consensus among middle class magistrates in England. Although some wholly rejected physical chastisement, others often believed that the wife deserved her beating.

The developing cult of domesticity which became so prominent in the nineteenth century reinforced the view that physical chastisement was inappropriate. Its roots can also be found in the Puritan sentiments of the seventeenth century and the notion of civility of the following century (Fletcher, 1995). Husbands were to be protectors; it was unmanly to beat your wife (Tomes, 1978; Harris, 1978). This could, on one hand, be used to reproach those husbands who violated the ideal; on the other, it perhaps blunted the reality of wife abuse among the middle classes.

In the decades following the founding of this nation, rejection of wife beating as a legitimate form of chastisement did not become the norm throughout society. Nor did it perhaps become so during the nineteenth century (Gordon, 1988; Clark, 1992). Nevertheless, Tomes (1978) suggests that the level of acceptable violence declined during the nineteenth century, at least in England. This was not necessarily just a matter of upper class mores. By the end of the eighteenth century, the rituals of public shaming so popular with the lower classes began to ridicule the husband who beat his wife, rather than the reverse (Fletcher, 1995; also Cobbe, 1994). In those American communities where middle class values affected behaviors, violence also become less acceptable (Pleck, 1987). Griswold (1982) in his study of rural divorce in California concurs. Nevertheless, among the urban working and lower classes, violence persisted.

In both countries, attitudes toward wife beating took on a particular class orientation (Tomes, 1978; Clark, 1992; Pleck, 1987). Class distinctions in England can be traced back to the seventeenth century debate. Fears of the lower classes, the rabble, was not new. In an age of urbanization and industrialization, they were accentuated (see also Pleck, 1987, for discussion of the levels of violence). The upper classes feared working class violence in all forms. By the middle of the nineteenth century, the English Parliament had intervened to increase criminal punishments for wife abuse (Clark, 1992; Tomes, 1978). In the United States, there was no federal legislation, but there was public debate that centered on the rule of men and the legal status of women.

Legal Status and the Law of Chastisement

To a degree, the legal status of married women following the American Revolution is in dispute. Scholars have suggested that the legal status of women in general, and married women in particular, actually declined in the decades following the founding of this country. This has been attributed in part to the widespread influence of Sir William Blackstone's *Commentaries on the Laws of England* in this country on the legal profession. He emphasized common law and the doctrine of coverture at the expense of equity (Beard, 1946). Although Blackstone lauded the social contract and declared freedom from assault to be a natural right, he did not extend it to wives (Clark, 1992). In addition to addressing the doctrine of coverture, Blackstone expressly referred to the husband's longstanding right to correct his wife in a reasonable manner.

Given the influence of Blackstone on American law, he has received his share of blame for perpetuating the right of chastisement. It is not to Blackstone, however, that we owe the infamous rule of thumb. According to Clark (1992) and Doggett (1992), this honor perhaps goes to one Sir Francis Buller, an English jurist, who in late 1782 reportedly coined the phrase. The rule condoned the use not simply of chastisement but of beating, specifying the weapon that could used. According to Clark (1992), it entered popular belief and reflected continued legal as well as societal ambivalence regarding physical correction.

The rule of thumb could be applied to criminal cases involving a charge of assault or battery, the offensive or unlawful touching of another. It could also be an evidentiary matter in divorce cases addressing cruelty. Those court records of the nineteenth century cited most often in regard to the rule, sometimes called the finger switch rule, are decisions of a few state Supreme Courts, most prominently in the south. Griswold (1982), however, relates that the California courts rejected the rule in 1857. Calvert (1974) found only seven cases occurring during the nineteenth century on the subject. This does not mean that more cases did not exist. High court records regarding chastisement only represent a small fraction of cases, those that were appealed. Significantly, appeals would likely occur only where a husband was convicted, and was willing to pay the cost of an appeal.

Mississippi is commonly regarded as the first state to recognize the rule of thumb in its own common law. In 1824, the Mississippi Supreme Court acknowledged that a husband did not have an "unlimited license" to commit assault and battery on his wife. The justices, however, did not reject the husband's authority to beat his wife with a "whip or rattan, no bigger " than his thumb (*Bradley v. State*, Walker 156, 157). In North Carolina, provocation by the wife was a defense to a charge of spousal battery until 1874 when the Supreme Court declared that the old doctrine that a husband would whip his wife was not law in the state (*State v. Oliver*, 70 N.C. 44). Nevertheless, the justices determined that from motives of public policy and protection of the "domestic circle" (45), courts should not intervene in family violence unless there existed permanent injury or extreme violence. They concluded, "(I)t is better to draw the curtain, shut out the public gaze, and leave the parties to forgive and forget" (45).

Common law and the rule of thumb represent one aspect of the American experience. In those states that more closely followed common law, particularly the southern states, Harris (1978) notes that wives were still more likely to be treated as property during the nineteenth century. Although the rule was eventually rejected, the courts reverted back to earlier experience. Government would only intrude in extreme cases. Working against this view were broad feminist challenges to the rule of the men in its many manifestations.

Feminism and Reform

By the early decades of the nineteenth century, women in America, predominantly from the middle and upper classes, sought reforms in many aspects of women's lives. The Seneca Falls Convention of 1848 with its *Declaration of Sentiments* was only one stop along this road. A major focus was elimination of the many remaining disabilities of coverture through various Married Women Property Acts. These laws sought to give married women an independent legal status. As the century progressed, married women in most states obtained the ability to contract, to manage and own both personal and real property, as well as the right to sue, and be sued (Lindgren and Taub, 1992). Economic independence became possible. To a degree, the notions of separate spheres and the cult of domesticity worked against these legal changes by encouraging middle class women to remain in their domestic sphere (Harris, 1978).

Feminist reformers recognized that women's lower legal status contributed to domestic violence (Clark, 1992). They also recognized that legal status was not just a matter of owning property. Laws giving wives the right to own, manage, and dispose of property would mean little in a home where a husband had the ultimate authority on his side, the ability to use physical force to obtain compliance with his wishes. This coercive potential had been recognized during the colonial period. Without legal control over his wife's property, a husband might be even more inclined to use force. Tomes (1978) suggests that much nineteenth century working class violence reflected male role insecurity. In 1854, Elizabeth Cady Stanton stood before the New York state legislature to demand justice for women. Among the grievances she cited was the husband's right to correct his wife, "to whip his wife with a rod not larger than his thumb, to shut her up in a room, and administer whatever moderate chastisement he may deem necessary to ensure obedience to his wishes" (cited in Lutz, 1940: 92). Feminists on both sides of the Atlantic focused on both the causes of wife beating and the options for abused wives.

By the last decades of the nineteenth century, feminist reformers possessed a clear vision of the reasons for wife beating. They addressed not only the dynamics of wife abuse but sought to root out its underlying causes. The foundation for wife beating, or more broadly chastisement, was firmly attributed to the rule of men. Frances Power Cobbe (1994:16) wrote in 1871 that "the common idea of the inferiority of women, and the special notion of the rights of husbands, form the undercurrent of feeling which induces a man, when for any reason he is infuriated, to wreak his violence on his wife." Challenges to the husband's authority–interfering, insubordination, willfulness–continued to be provocations (Clark, 1992). Feminists, however, recognized these not as justifications but as excuses that had existed for centuries. Beyond the rule of husbands, they sought to understand the sources of marital discord that led to violence.

Two primary sources of tension emerged: the consumption of alcohol and financial disputes. Both, in fact, had long been reflected in the documentation of criminal and civil cases. Although feminist reformers focused largely on working class violence, they also recognized that the middle classes were not free from marital violence. In working class families and the laboring poor, economic factors in particular heightened the possibility of marital tension. Cobbe (1994) and Gordon (1988) provide examples of women beaten for attempting to secure food and clothing for their children, for requesting a greater allowance, or for reproaching husbands who spent their wages on drink. Women who worked often faired no better. In 1877, Ezra Heywood chided (8), "We form societies to prevent cruelty to dumb animals, but horses and dogs are better fed and lodged in our cities, than thousands of working women."

It is perhaps not surprising that temperance was supported by women's groups campaigning for social purity as well as suffragette feminists demanding an independent legal status (Gordon, 1988; Pleck, 1987). Drinking was an assertion of a husband's privilege (Gordon, 1988). Cobbe (1994) recognized drunkenness among the laboring classes as a primary catalyst for physical abuse. She also acknowledged that intoxication could be a problem for both husband and wife leading to mutual combat. Gordon (1988) describes the epidemic problem of drunkenness among Boston's working classes during the last decades of the nineteenth century.

The Limitations of Legal Independence

For most married women, newly won legal independence remained a legal fiction. Enforcing independence required a financial ability sufficient for access to the courts. Control over wages and marital finances often remained in the hands of the husband. Other vestiges of a husband's power in marriage also remained. At common law, in the marriage contract a wife "consented" to sexual intercourse. The Married Women's Property Acts did not alter this aspect of marriage although feminist and social purity reformers attacked sexual abuses and excesses in marriage (Pleck, 1987). The legal system continued to support this implied consent, another legal fiction, by refusing to acknowledge that a husband could rape his wife. (For a detailed discussion of the husband's right to his wife's body, see Shanley, 1989.) Control of procreation also remained behind closed doors. Religious doctrine advanced the sanctity of procreation and condemned attempts to intrude into the family (McLaren, 1990). While wives perhaps legally had little control over their bodies, in reality women had long sought to regulate family size (see, for example, McLaren, 1990).

Feminists particularly recognized that wives needed protection and the ability to escape escalating violence. In the United States there was "no major campaign specifically directed against cruelty to women" (Gordon, 1988: 253). As noted above, feminists largely addressed the issue through the broader debate on the legal status of women. According to Gordon (1988), although severe cases of wife beating could result in criminal complaints, in the nineteenth century women were more likely to file complaints for nonsupport. Financial support could be seen as an entitlement. Beating, on the other hand, remained a fact of life. In some states, statutes were enacted not only recognizing the husband's duty to support his wife but criminalizing his failure to do so. Okun (1986) suggests, however, that the standard for proving a husband's failure to support was onerous, if not impossible.

Access to Divorce

As the nineteenth century progressed, divorce laws expanded as an option for abused wives. Although the law changed dramatically, such change was not uniform. Absolute divorce began to replace legal separation as the most common form of dissolution. By the end of the century, judicial divorce became the norm. Grounds for divorce and legal separation were also broadened in many states. Although not all states recognized physical cruelty, those that did tended to make it easier to prove. In several states, inhuman treatment replaced life threatening injury. In addition, some states recognized verbal and mental cruelty as grounds for divorce. Sexual cruelty or excess also came to be recognized. By the middle of the century, a growing number of states granted divorce on the grounds of intemperance or habitual drunkenness. Several Western states added willful neglect. (See, generally, Riley, 1991; Pleck, 1987; Griswold, 1982.)

Both the number and rate of divorces increased during the nineteenth century. According to Riley (1991), in the North and Middle Atlantic states, people increasingly regarded divorce as a citizen's democratic right. The southern states saw the least change. Divorce became most common in the Western states and territories. In the post-Civil War period, divorce rates increased across the country, but most significantly in the West. (For detailed discussions of the statistics and rates, see Riley, 1991 and Pleck, 1987). Some western states became known as divorce mills, providing quick and inexpensive divorces. Critics of this trend bemoaned the end of the family (Riley, 1991). Although the uncertainty and isolation of frontier life may explain some of the growth in the West, it does not account for continued high rates in settled areas. In addition, liberal divorce laws perhaps do not fully account for the rates. Scholars such as Griswold (1982) and Riley (1991) point to the additional factor of rising expectations. New generations of married couples were more likely to expect a marital partnership based on affection and respect, and, perhaps, less likely to be so tolerant of abusive behavior.

The existence of more liberal divorce statutes did not necessarily mean that the courts were always receptive to their use (Okun, 1986). In cases of extreme cruelty, wives could still be required to show that they were blameless (e.g., Peterson, 1991). Legal interpretation of the grounds for divorce fell to the courts. Petrik's (1987) study of divorce in Montana during the late 1800s revealed that in the middle class town of Helena during the 1880s, a wife could obtain a divorce based on mental cruelty or one instance of physical abuse while in the working class town of Butte, trial judges required a pattern of physical violence. In most cases, divorce remained both costly and public. The petitioner had to hire an attorney, secure witnesses, and answer very personal questions. Many women worked of necessity and could ill afford a divorce. (See, for example, Peterson, 1991; Petrik, 1987.) In addition, liberalized divorce laws often did not provide for adequate support or alimony.

By the end of the nineteenth century, among feminists and reformers, there was a subtle shift away from concentrating on the rule of husbands to recognizing another dynamic–the marital relationship (Gordon, 1988, Pleck, 1987). This shift was encouraged by reformist emphasis on the family (Gordon, 1988). It was also encouraged by the continued failure of legal remedies, and the practical need to protect wives. Most wives, then as now, simply wanted the violence to stop.

A NEW ERA?

There is no fine line between the nineteenth and twentieth centuries in regard to wife abuse. By the end of the nineteenth century, the rule of thumb had been discredited in law. As in the past, prosecutions for spousal assault or battery occurred occasionally but generally only in extreme cases (Gordon, 1988). No state specifically legislated against wife beating. By the early twentieth century, it was common for police departments and social service agencies to intervene in matters of family violence. However, arrests remained rare (Gordon, 1988). Complaints about police indifference and bias are reminiscent of more recent decades (Gordon, 1988).

Other legal protections remained limited. Although civil lawsuits for injuries resulting from battery became recognized in many states, abused wives did not benefit from this. Most state legislatures continued to provide for immunity in marriage: a wife could not sue her husband. Only in recent decades of this century has spousal immunity been rejected (Calvert, 1974). Divorce law also continued to require evidence of fault in most states until the 1960s, and such statutes were left to judicial interpretation.

In the community, divorce remained stigmatized. The woman became a divorcee, the brunt of gossip and ostracism. Being a single mother was especially objectionable (Gordon, 1988). Community norms and religious doctrines were also slow to change. Marriage vows in both civil and religious ceremonies, until recent decades of the twentieth century, required the husband to cherish and love his wife while she promised to obey him.

In addressing wife abuse, feminist reformers were largely replaced by female professionals working in community and social services agencies.

The caseworkers of Gordon's study (1988: 252) addressed spousal violence indirectly, in their focus on the "peaceful family" (Gordon, 1988: 252). Spousal abuse was seen to result from mutual conflict revolving around money, work, sex, alcohol, and changing expectations. (For a detailed discussion of the dynamics of changing expectations in the family, see Gordon, 1988.) This focus was encouraged by new disciplines or professions, in particular social workers and psychologists who concentrated on counseling individuals in the family. According to Gordon (1988: 264), wife beating, particularly involving alcohol abuse, tended to become a "male foible"; it was seen as resulting from a husband's loss of control. Some social workers tried to ignore wife beating (Gordon, 1988). It became just one of those things that happened in marriage (Gordon, 1988).

Working class mothers were increasingly caught in a double bind. They were criticized for being economically dependent and unemployed; at the same time, those who held jobs were chastised for working and neglecting their domestic duties (Gordon, 1988). Pleck (1987) adds that changes from social caseworker to psychiatric caseworker beginning in the 1920s further altered the profession's focus. The therapeutic ideal favored family intervention by psychiatric professionals, not the police. Family sociologists also saw physical abuse as an aspect of "domestic discord" (Pleck, 1987). Among professionals, masochism increasingly explained why abused women stayed and why they provoked the beating (Gordon, 1988). Wife blaming persisted in a new guise.

By the 1960s, a new women's movement and a new feminism challenged old stereotypes and attitudes. To a degree, the earlier battles had succeeded in women gaining political, economic, and social power. Marriage had become a more equal relationship. Yet, wives continued to be raped by their husbands without recourse. Battered women remained secluded behind closed doors whether those doors secured an isolated homestead, a squalid tenement, or a fashionable townhouse. It is the protection of these women that was the concern in the many grass roots movements to provide shelter and services that began in the 1970s. Significantly, such movements appeared at the same time in England and this country (for a detailed discussion, see Dobash and Dobash, 1992). These were followed by new legal interventions including civil protection orders, as well as social science research.

CONCLUSION

Although the adage "history repeats itself" is commonly criticized, most often by historians themselves, it cannot be denied that the stories of wife abuse in American history sound like a broken record. The same arguments, justifications, methods, and options recur again and again. In her study, Pleck

(1987) suggests that this history reflects an ebb and flow where in three historical periods–early Puritan New England, the last decades of the 1800s, and the current era beginning in the 1950s–family violence became a matter of public policy, to a degree influenced by perceived levels of violence. Each was preceded or accompanied by a period of religious, political, or economic revolution. The first two eras of attention were followed by disinterest and reinforcement of old views. Nevertheless, change did occur over time in attitudes, and law. Efforts were made to alleviate the harshest forms of marital violence.

In any given period prior to our present time, including those where family violence was a public matter, none of the resources available to wives resisting physical violence provided adequate protection. Divorce and legal separation continued to be costly and very public. The courts were also often unsympathetic. Criminal complaints, like civil actions, largely remained a last resort. Gordon (1988) notes that the final option earlier in this century was desertion, like abandonment in prior eras. Child welfare agencies eventually became a part of direct government intervention when children were involved, but women were as likely to be blamed as protected. Women, of course, could fight back, but they were more often the losers. It remains to be seen how our present day experience will be retold.

Pleck (1987) and Gordon (1988) emphasize that true reform against family violence requires that it be acknowledged as a public issue, not a private matter; as a social problem, not a personal one. How much government intervention should occur remains the subject of debate. Some feminists caution against using the coercive power of government to intervene in the home (Martin, 1993). Amussen (1992) and Pleck (1987) suggest that the public nature of domestic violence limited it in seventeenth century England and the New England colonies respectively. Yet, in such communities, there remained acceptable levels of violence in society, in the home. This dynamic continues. According to Pleck (1987), society remains bound by the notion of the Family Ideal–ideas of conjugal rights, family privacy and stability.

The ideal remains framed by patriarchy–the rule of men bolstered by law, society, and culture has sustained the subordination of women and the subjection of married women. Yet, the tapestry is not completed. Middle and upper class wife abuse remains to be more closely studied. The contributions, and failures, of feminism also require closer examination. Regional variations need to be considered. Local history from long forgotten journals to oral remembrances can shed new light on domestic violence in American society. Recently, historical research on women in prison adds another dimension to the choices of abused women (e.g., Butler, 1997). Literature also can be revealing. Graulich (1987) exposes a counterpoint to the pioneer family of Ma and Pa Ingalls in her review of four western authors of the early twentieth century. These women reveal not only their own stories of violence but suggest that wife abuse violence was commonplace in the western United States. While it can never be stated to a certainty how widespread spousal brutality has been in history, it can be agreed that it has been to a degree tolerated, moreover condoned. In the face of such acceptance, government intervention has been only partially successful. These are lessons to be learned as society tackles the complex problem of wife beating in the last years of the twentieth century. The fact that husbands are less likely to claim a right to chastise does not mean that they have abandoned the use physical violence to maintain control. The subordination of women, of wives, lingers as an ideology.

REFERENCES

Amussen, Bonnie Dwyer (1994) "'Being Stirred to Much Unquietness:' Violence and Domestic Violence in Early Modern England." *Journal of Women's History*, 6: 70-89.

Anderson, Bonnie S. and Judith Zinsser (1988) *A History of Their Own: Women in European History from Prehistory to the Present*; 2 Vols. New York: Harper and Row.

St. Augustine (1977) From "The City of God," In Rosemary Agonito (ed.), *History of Ideas on Women*. New York: Perigee Press, pp. 73-80.

Bailey, Abigail Abbot (1989) *Religion and Domestic Violence in Early New England: The Memoirs of Abigail Abbot Bailey*. Ann Taves (ed.). Bloomington: Indiana University Press.

Beattie, J.M. (1986). *Crime and the Courts in England 1660-1800*. Princeton: Princeton University Press.

Beard, Mary (1946) *Women as Force in History*. New York: Macmillan.

Benson, Mary Sumner, ed. (1935; 1966 ed.) *Women in Eighteenth-Century America: A Study of Opinion and Social Usage*. Port Washington, NY: Kennikat Press.

Butler, Anne M. (1997) *Gendered Justice in the American West: Women Prisoners in Men's Penitentiaries*. Urbana: University of Illinois Press.

Calvert, Robert (1974) "Criminal and Civil Liability in Husband-Wife Assaults," In Suzanne K. Steinmetz and Murray A. Straus (eds.), *Violence in the Family*. New York: Harper & Row, pp. 88-91.

Clark, Anna (1992) "Humanity or Justice? Wifebeating and the Law in the Eighteenth and Nineteenth Centuries," In Carol Smart (ed.), *Regulating Womanhood: Historical Essays on Marriage, Motherhood and Sexuality*. London: Routledge, pp. 187-206.

Cobbe, Frances Power (1994) "Wife-Torture in England," In M. Roberts and T. Mizula (eds.) *The Wives: The Rights of Married Women*. London: Routledge.

Davidson, Terry (1977) "Wifebeating: A Recurring Phenomenon Throughout History," In Maria Roy (ed.) *Battered Women: A Psychological Study of Domestic Violence*. New York: Van Nostrand Reinhold, pp. 2-23.

Davis, Elisabeth Gould (1971) *The First Sex*. New York: Putnam.

Dobash, R. Emerson and Russell P. Dobash (1992) *Women, Violence, and Social Change.* London: Routledge.

Doggett, Maeve E. (1992) *Marriage, Wife-Beating and the Law in Victorian England.* London: Weidenfeld and Nicholson.

Fletcher, Anthony (1995) *Gender, Sex and Subordination in England 1500-1800.* New Haven: Yale University Press.

Frey, Sylvia R. and Marian J. Morton, eds. (1986) *New World, New Roles: A Documentary History of Women in Pre-Industrial America.* New York: Greenwood Press.

Gordon, Linda (1988) *Heroes of Their Own Lives: Politics and History of Family Violence, Boston 1880-1960.* New York: Viking Press.

Graulich, Melody (1987). "Violence Against Women: Power Dynamics in Literature of the Western Family," In Susan Armitage and Elizabeth Johnson (eds.), *The Women's West.* Norman: University of Oklahoma Press, pp. 111-126.

Griswold, Robert L. (1982) *Family and Divorce in California, 1850-1890.* Albany: State University of New York Press.

Harris, Barbara (1978) *Beyond Her Sphere: Women and the Professions in American History.* Westport, Connecticut; Greenwood Press.

Heywood, Ezra (1877, reprint 1974) "Uncivil Liberty: An Essay to Show the Injustice and Impolicy of Ruling Women Without Her Consent," In *Sex and Equality: Women in America: From Colonial Times to the 20th Century.* New York: Arno Press.

Hunt, Margaret R. (1995) "'The Great Danger She Had Reason to Believe She Was In,' Wifebeating in the Eighteenth Century," In Valerie Frith (ed.), *Women & History: Voices of Early Modern England.* Toronto: Coach House Press, pp. 81-10.

Ingram, Martin (1987) *Church Courts, Sex and Marriage in England, 1570-1640.* Cambridge: Cambridge University Press.

Leyser, Henrietta (1995) *Medieval Women: A Social History of Women in England 450-1500.* New York: St. Martin's Press.

Lindgren, J. Ralph and Nadine Taub (1993) *The Law of Sex Discrimination.* Minneapolis/St. Paul: West Publishing.

Lutz, Alma (1940, reprint 1974) *Created Equal: A Biography of Elizabeth Cady Stanton.* New York: Octagon Books.

Martin, Margaret (1993) "Battered Women and the Criminal Justice System." *Odyssey,* July: 90-96.

McLaren, Angus (1990) *A History of Contraception from Antiquity to the Present Day.* Oxford: Blackwell.

Okun, Lewis (1986) *Women Abuse: Facts Replacing Myths.* New York: State University of New York Press.

Peterson, David (1991) "Physically Violent Husbands of the 1890s and Their Resources." *Journal of Family Violence,* 6:1-15.

Petrik, Paula (1987) "If She be Content: The Development of Montana Divorce Law, 1865-1907." *Western Historical Quarterly,* 18: 261-291.

Pleck, Elizabeth (1987) *Domestic Tyranny: The Making of American Social Policy Against Family Violence from Colonial Times to the Present.* New York and Oxford: Oxford University Press.

Riley, Glenda (1991) *Divorce: An American Tradition*. New York and Oxford: Oxford University Press.

Salmon, Marylynn (1986) *Women and the Law of Property in Early America*. Chapel Hill: University of North Carolina Press.

Shanley, Mary Lyndon (1989) *Feminism, Marriage, and the Law in Victorian England, 1850-1895*. Princeton: Princeton University Press.

Speth, Linda E. and Alison Duncan Hirsch (1983) *Women, Family, and Community in Colonial America: Two Perspectives*. New York: The Haworth Press, Inc.

Tomes, Nancy (1978) "A 'Torrent of Abuse': Crimes of Violence Between Working-Class Men and Women in London 1840-1875." *Journal of Social History*, 11:328-345.

Treckel, Paula (1996) *To Comfort the Heart: Women in Seventeenth-Century America*. New York, Twayne Publishers; London, Prentice Hall International.

Ulrich, Laurel Thatcher (1982) *Good Wives: Image and Reality in the Lives of Women in Northern New England, 1650-1750*. New York: Alfred P. Knopf.

Woloch, Nancy, ed. (1992) *Early American Women: A Documentary History, 1600-1900*. Belmont, CA: Wadsworth Publishing.

CASES CITED

Bradley v. State, Walker 156 (Mississippi, 1824).
State v. Oliver, 70 N.C. 44 (North Carolina, 1874).

Protecting Battered Women:
Latest Trends in Civil Legal Relief

Catherine F. Klein
Leslye E. Orloff

SUMMARY. Domestic violence is a major societal problem that affects millions of people. The American legal system is attempting to assist victims of domestic violence by designing laws that offer various types of protection. The civil laws have been expanded to provide protection to more people, such as dating partners, same-sex couples, and people who offer help to victims. In addition, a victim of domestic violence can seek a particularized form of relief, designed for their specific situation. The laws will vary between jurisdictions, but the movement is towards more complete and effective laws that assist people who are in violent situations. *[Article copies available for a fee from The Haworth Document Delivery Service: 1-800-342-9678. E-mail address: getinfo@haworthpressinc.com]*

Catherine F. Klein, JD, Associate Professor and Director, The Families and the Law Clinic, Columbus School of Law, The Catholic University of America, and Director of Catholic University's clinical domestic violence program since 1981.

Leslye E. Orloff, JD, Founder of Clinica Legal Latina, the domestic violence program at Ayuda, Inc., a community based legal services program for immigrant and refugee women in Washington, DC; Ms. Orloff has been representing immigrant battered women since 1983, and is currently Ayuda's Director of Program Development responsible for domestic violence policy work on both local and national levels.

The authors wish to express their gratitude to Jennifer Marino, third year law student at the Columbus School of Law, The Catholic University of America, for her assistance in completing this article.

[Haworth co-indexing entry note]: "Protecting Battered Women: Latest Trends in Civil Legal Relief." Klein, Catherine F. and Leslye E. Orloff. Co-published simultaneously in *Women & Criminal Justice* (The Haworth Press, Inc.) Vol. 10, No. 2, 1999, pp. 29-47; and: *Women and Domestic Violence: An Interdisciplinary Approach* (ed: Lynette Feder) The Haworth Press, Inc., 1999, pp. 29-47. Single or multiple copies of this article are available for a fee from The Haworth Document Delivery Service [1-800-342-9678, 9:00 a.m. - 5:00 p.m. (EST). E-mail address: getinfo@haworthpressinc.com].

INTRODUCTION

Family and intimate violence is a major societal problem that poses a significant health risk to millions of women and children in the United States each year. In an effort to combat this problem the American judicial system has increased legal protection to family violence victims and significantly enhanced criminal punishment of abusers.

State and federal domestic violence laws are premised on an understanding that a two-pronged legal approach of pursuing the civil and criminal processes concurrently is necessary if legal intervention is to effectively curb domestic violence. First, battered women must be able to obtain and enforce the legal relief they need to end the abusive relationship. This civil form of legal relief will usually provide protection from ongoing violence, legal permission to remain in their home, legal custody of their children, child support, and the ability to obtain any additional relief necessary to stop ongoing violence in each particular relationship. Second, the domestic violence incident must be handled as a crime. Those who abuse family members should be punished in the same way as those who commit crimes against strangers. By punishing perpetrators of domestic violence in the criminal justice system, the legal system is providing the second step that is needed to effectively reduce the amount of domestic violence incidents.

This two-pronged approach allows the state to punish perpetrators of domestic violence for their crimes in the criminal courts in a case controlled by state prosecutors, while simultaneously allowing abuse victims to receive the particularized civil relief they need by filing for a protection order in a civil or family court. These two systems are separate options, so battered women and other family violence victims may file for, obtain and enforce civil protection orders whether or not the abuser is prosecuted in criminal court. This provides abuse victims with protection before the abuse has come to the attention of the police or prosecutors. While both processes are equally important to victims of domestic violence, this paper will focus on the civil aspect of domestic violence relief, focusing particularly on civil protection orders.

WHO IS ENTITLED TO SEEK A PROTECTION ORDER

In all states there are specific relationship requirements that must be met before a person is eligible to obtain a protection order. Almost all states grant protection orders between spouses, ex-spouses, and family members, defined as persons related by blood, marriage, or adoption. In addition, most states allow for protection orders between people who are unmarried and living together as spouses, including same sex couples, or between two people who share a child in common.

There is a growing trend among states to grant protection orders between people who are in a dating relationship (Klein & Orloff, 1993). Since dating violence is a serious problem among high school and college students, this is a positive development that is being followed by state legislatures throughout the country. In many cases, teens and adolescents are experiencing the same abusive pattern as adults in abusive relationships experience (Ganley, 1992). Studies have found that between 20% and 67% of teens had experienced some form of physical violence in their dating relationship (Morrell, 1984; O'Keefe, 1986; Rouse, 1988). In addition it has been found that more than half of students who witnessed violence in their home have been involved in an abusive relationship (O'Keefe, 1986).

In light of these statistics, it is important that states protect people in a dating relationship by enabling them to petition for civil protection orders. This not only offers protection to the victim, but teaches the offender, at a young age, that physical violence toward an intimate will not be tolerated, and will be punished if it continues. The definition of dating varies from state to state. Some statutes consider a romantic relationship, without sexual intimacy (N.H. Rev. Stat. Ann. § 173-B:1 (1992); N.D. Cent. Code § 14.07.1-01 (1993); Wash. Rev. Code Ann. § 26.50.010 (2)-(3) (1993)), while other states take a more strict approach requiring an engagement or an intimate sexual relationship (R.I. Gen. Laws § 8-8.1-1 (1993); W. Va. Code § 48-2A-2 (1993)).

Another important issue is treatment of minors. People under the age of 18, if emancipated, can seek a protection order against a family member or a dating partner in a growing number of states (Ala. Code § 30-5-2(2) (1989); Ind. Code Ann § 34-4-5.1-1 (1992); La. Rev. Stat. Ann. 46:2132 (4)(1982); N.J. Stat. Ann. § 2c:25-18 (1992); 23 Pa. Cons. Stat. Ann. § 6102 (1992); R.I. Gen Laws § 15-15-1 (supp. 1993); Wyo. Stat. § 35-21-102(a) (1)(1993)). If the child is not emancipated, most courts will issue a protection order based on a petition filed by an adult on behalf of the child. In 1994 the National Council of Juvenile and Family Court Judges issued a Model Code On Domestic Violence ("Model Code") recommended for adoption by all states. The Model Code, which was developed by a team of judicial experts working in consultation with domestic violence advocates, prosecutors, criminal defense attorneys, and state legislators, proposes a progressive uniform model legal approach to curbing domestic violence to be adopted by all states (National Council of Juvenile and Family Court Judges, 1994). The commentary in the Model Code states that minor victims can petition for a protection order on their own or they can have a adult petition on their behalf (Id. § 301.2).

In addition, in a growing number of states, a protection order can be issued against a minor. In *Diehl v. Drummond* (1989) an early reported decision on this issue, a civil protection order was issued against a sixteen year-old. However, the court clarified that any enforcement of the order must occur in juvenile court, which is designed to protect the rights of juvenile defendants (Id.).

Research demonstrates that the batterer's violence can extend to people who are attempting to assist the victim, whether the person offering help is an attorney, friend or relative (Ganley, 1992). There are a few states that now offer protection to people who attempt to offer refuge and/or aid to victims of domestic violence (see, e.g., Haw. Rev. Stat. § 586-4 (1992); 725 ILCS 5/112A-4 (1993)). These states recognize the importance of offering protection to persons who offer refuge to abuse victims, by allowing them to be included in a protection order. This will help to ensure that people will not be hesitant in helping abused persons. A few other states have case law that also support this innovative relief (see, e.g., *Caldwell v. Coppola*, 1990).

TYPICAL GROUNDS FOR A PROTECTION ORDER

In order for a person to obtain a civil protection order there needs to be some act, usually criminal, committed by the alleged abuser. Conduct that is considered sufficient to obtain a protection order will vary among state statutes. Assault and battery are the most common offenses on which a protection order will be based (Klein & Orloff, 1993). Examples of this are striking and kicking the petitioner (*Parkhurst v. Parkhurst*, 1990), yanking the petitioner's hair (*Pierson v. Pierson*, 1990), and attempting to push the petitioner's face in the toilet (*Sielski v. Sielski*, 1990). A protection order may be issued based on physical abuse whether or not the conduct resulted in visible physical injury to the abuse victim. In most states a protection order can also be awarded based on sexual assault, threats, attempts to harm, and damage to property (Klein & Orloff, 1993).

There are several states that are now beginning to issue protection orders based on threatening and controlling behaviors such as harassment, stalking and emotional abuse (see, e.g., N.J. Stat. Ann. § 2C:25-19 (1993); N.M. Stat. Ann. § 40-13-2 (1993); N.Y. Fam. Ct. Act. Law § 812(1) (1994)). By responding to these behaviors quickly the court may be able to prevent any further and more violent abuse. Harassment is used as a mechanism by batterers to control their victims, so by including harassment as a ground for a protection order, the statute will provide the victims with a tool to stop the violence before it escalates. Among the states that include harassment as grounds for protection, the definitions vary, but may include following the victim, threatening the victim, driving around the victim's home, moving near the victim's home and calling the victim repeatedly at work (Klein & Orloff, 1993).

Stalking initially begins as annoying, but legal behavior. However, it often escalates into dangerous and violent behavior (National Institute of Justice, 1993). If protection orders are granted to stalking victims when the harassing behavior starts, then it is predicted that future violence may be prevented (Id.). In almost all states stalking is now considered criminal behavior, so victims stalked by family members should now be able to obtain a protection order. A few states explicitly grant the court authority to issue a protection order based on evidence of stalking (N.M. Stat. Ann. § 40-13-2 (1993); N.J. Stat. Ann. § 2C:25-19 (1993); Okla. Stat. Ann. tit. 22, § 60.1(1992); R.I. Gen. Laws §§ 11-59-2 to-3(1993)). Therefore, victims stalked by family members or intimate partners may ask courts to use their authority to issue protection orders based on stalking behavior.

Emotional abuse is another behavior that is being recognized by some states as a basis for a protection order (see, e.g., Del. Code Ann. tit. 10, § 945 (1992); Haw. Rev. Stat. § 586-1 (1993); N.M. Stat. Ann. § 40-13-2(c)(2) (1993); N.Y. Fam. Ct. Act § 821-1(a) (1994)). Examples of emotional abuse are threats, insults and degrading comments. This is a significant component in the array of behaviors a batterer uses to maintain control over the victim. In 1994, U.S. immigration law recognized that emotional abuse can amount to extreme cruelty, which is a form of spousal abuse (Immigration and Nationality Act, 1996). International laws, agreements and treaties have long recognized the importance of curbing and sanctioning emotional as well as physical abuse. Therefore it is important that more jurisdictions include emotional abuse as a ground for a protection order.

An additional way a batterer can maintain control over a victim is to interfere with the victim's personal liberty. Some states are beginning to issue protection orders based on this controlling behavior (Conn. Gen. Stat. Ann. § 46b-14 (1993); Del. Code. Ann. tit. 10 § 945 (1993); Ga. Code Ann. § 19-13-1 (1993); 725 ILCS 5/112A-3 (1993); Nev. Rev. Stat. Ann. § 33.018 (1993); Vt. Stat. Ann. tit. 15, § 1104 (1992)). Examples of interfering with a person's freedom can be physically preventing a person from leaving the home or calling the police or locking a person out of the home and threatening to physically remove the person from the property (see, e.g., *In re Marriage of Blitstein*, 1991; *Wagner v. Wagner*, 1980).

EMERGENCY OR TEMPORARY PROTECTION ORDERS

In most jurisdictions temporary protection orders are available to victims of domestic violence as immediate relief, through an *ex parte* hearing. In an *ex parte* hearing one party appears before the judge to seek emergency relief, without notifying the opposing party. This provides the most immediate and temporary relief to a victim of domestic violence. In the *Matter of Baker*

(1992), the Minnesota Supreme Court articulated an understanding that has been uniformly adopted by legislators and courts across the country and is repeated in the Model Code. The Court stated that requiring notice would inhibit the abused person's ability to obtain immediate relief, and may place the party in further danger.

Most jurisdictions require that the petitioner show good cause, probable cause or reasonable belief that she is in imminent danger as the standard to obtain a temporary protection order, *ex parte*. This basically means that she must show by a preponderance of the evidence, more than a 50% probability, that she or her child is in imminent harm. Usually a victim can present evidence of recent violence or serious threats to meet the required standard. Visible bruises or injuries are not required to obtain a temporary order. *Ex parte* temporary protection orders are issued on the sworn testimony or affidavit of the petitioner and may be issued in most jurisdictions at any time of day. Progressive jurisdictions allow police officers to contact a judge and issue emergency temporary protection orders when a domestic violence crime has occurred (National Council of Family and Juvenile Court Judges, 1994). A majority of jurisdictions allow the same remedies for temporary protection orders as they do for civil protection orders (Klein & Orloff, 1993).

WHAT REMEDIES ARE AVAILABLE

There are various forms of remedies that an abused person may seek in a civil protection order. Most states allow courts to interpret the protection order statutes broadly. Consequently, each judge can create a remedy that is specifically suited to each individual victim's needs. Before petitioning a court for a protection order, victims may need help in identifying all the relief they would ideally need to stop the violence and settle issues that might otherwise become areas of continuing conflict between themselves and their abuser. Too often victims do not get the relief they need because they are unaware of the possible remedies to which they may be entitled.

In almost every state, the civil protection order statute includes a catch-all remedy provision (Klein & Orloff, 1993). These provisions can be used to fashion a specific remedy for each individual victim of abuse. Courts have ordered various kinds of relief under the catch-all provisions, such as compensatory and punitive damages (*Sielski v. Sielski*, 1992), transferring real estate (*Rayan v. Dykeman*, 1990), and ordering child support (*Powell v. Powell*, 1988). Another form of relief that may be ordered under the catch-all provision, which is very important to immigrant women, is that the abuser be ordered to not withdraw any papers that were filed with the Immigration and Naturalization Service, or that he participate in any required INS proceedings regarding the victim. The Model Code and most state statutes include such catch-all provisions stating that the court can "order such other relief as it deems necessary to provide for the safety and welfare of the petitioner and any designated family or household member" (National Council, § 306(h), 1994). Because every domestic violence case is different, it is important that courts have the latitude to design creative and particularized relief aimed at stopping the violence in each individual relationship that comes before the court.

In addition to giving judges discretion to order any relief necessary, all states statutes contain a list of specific remedies that may be included in protection orders. The most common remedies available in every jurisdiction are prohibitions against further abuse, stay-away provisions and no contact provisions. In all states, courts can order the respondent to refrain from entering the victim's residence, school, property or place of employment, as well as any other place that is specified in the order, including places that the victim and her family members frequent regularly (see, e.g., N.J. ST. 2C: 25-29 (b)(6), 1993). In addition, the court has the power to order the defendant to refrain from contacting the victim in any way. The defendant can be ordered not to initiate communication through an agent, or with any person whom contacting would likely cause annoyance or alarm to the victim (Id.). This includes, but is not limited to, communications via mail, facsimile, electronic mail, or telephone.

Courts in all states may also include no further abuse clauses in protection orders. These clauses are essential to include in every protection order, and should clearly state what the abuser is forbidden to do. Without this clause, enforcement of protection orders becomes very difficult. No abuse clauses can prohibit behaviors such as harassing, assaulting, intimidating and threatening the abused person. Other family members, especially children, can and should be included in the no further abuse clause of a protection order. Batterers frequently try to maintain control over their victims by threatening harm to children or family members, so it is crucial to include such individuals in the no further abuse provision (*Stuckey v. Stuckey*, 1989). All state statutes allow victims, who continue to reside with their abusers, to obtain protection orders containing only a no further abuse clause, giving the victim legal protection to help end the violent acts.

Providing the victim with monetary relief is also an important provision that is included in domestic violence statutes in a majority of jurisdictions (see, e.g., Ala. Code § 30-5-7(a)(5), (1993); Ind. Code Ann. § 34-4-5.1(a)(3), (1993); N.Y. Fam. Ct. Act § 842, (1994); P.R. Laws Ann. Tit. 8, § 664, (1990); Wyo. Stat. § 35-21-105(b),(1993)). Moreover, in *Powell v. Powell* (1988), the District of Columbia Court of Appeals held that monetary relief can be awarded to the abused if it is an effective means to end the violence, even if the state statute does not explicitly authorize monetary relief. Many victims of domestic violence remain in the abusive relationship because of the economic control that the batterer had over the abused. By awarding monetary relief the court is helping to end the controlling behavior, foster economic independence, thus making it possible for some victims to leave an abusive relationship.

The primary form of monetary relief issued by protection order courts across the country is child support. Most state statutes explicitly authorize child support in their protection order remedies, but in those states that do not, child support may be awarded under the catch-all provision of the statute. Additionally, in Pennsylvania, the court can direct the respondent to pay for reasonable damages and losses that are a result of the abuse (23 Pa.C.S.A. § 6108(a)(8), (1991)).

In many states, statutes explicitly allow courts to make decisions regarding property when deciding a protection order case. It is important that property issues be handled by the court, at least on a temporary basis, to prevent the victim from having to interact immediately with her abuser to settle property disputes. Some state statutes specifically state that a protection order will not affect title to personal property (see, e.g., Del. Code Ann. tit. 10 § 949, (1993); N.H. Rev. Stat. Ann. § 173-B:4(II), (1990); N.J. Stat Ann. § 2C: 25-29b, (1993); N.M. Stat Ann. § 40-13-5, (1993)), while most states allow a court to grant exclusive possession of personal property to one party (see, e.g., Ga. Code Ann. § 19-13-4, (1993); La. Rev. Stat. Ann. § 46:2135(A) (2), (1982)).

It is important for the judge to resolve these property issues in order to reduce the chances of future conflict between the parties. If the court makes a decision regarding the property, it lowers the likelihood of contact between the parties, which can help prevent future violence (Walker, 1984). One study found that 59% of batterers destroy or damage personal property of the victim, so it is necessary to allow the court to make a decision regarding property issues in a civil protection order (Follingstad, 1990).

Virtually all jurisdictions authorize the court to grant to the petitioner the exclusive possession of the family home, and to evict the abuser from the home (see, e.g., N.J. Stat. Ann. 2C:25-29(b)(2), (1993); N.D. Cent. Code § 14-07.1-02.4.f (1993)). This award of possession does not affect the title or interest in the property or any other real property held jointly by the parties (Id.). In addition, if it is not possible for the victim to remain in the residence, then the court can order the respondent to pay for the victim's rent at another residence if the court finds that the respondent has a duty to support the petitioner (N.J. Stat. Ann. § 2C:25-29(b)(2), (1993)).

Increasingly state protection order statutes include provisions prohibiting the abuser from owning or possessing a weapon. Courts also invoke the catch-all remedy provisions in protection order statutes to order this important relief. Under the Model Code, law enforcement officers are authorized to seize all weapons that were alleged to have been used or were threatened to be used in domestic or family violence cases. In addition, the Model Code states that a weapon may be seized if it is in plain view of the officer or was discovered pursuant to a lawful search (National Council, § 207, 1994).

The federal law, however, has a slightly different approach. The new law, enacted in 1996, amends the 1994 Crime Bill to state that any person convicted of any crime that involves an act of domestic violence is prohibited from owning or possessing a handgun, regardless of whether the crime is classified as a felony or misdemeanor (18 U.S.C. § 922(g)). This provision applies to law enforcement officials. The 1994 legislation already stated that if a person has a civil protection order against them, they are prohibited from owning or possessing a firearm. Currently, this provision does not apply to law enforcement officials (Id.). Under this federal law, the respondent can be prosecuted for simply possessing a firearm during the period that the protection order is in effect. The respondent does not have to violate the protection order before he can be prosecuted for possessing a firearm. This law also makes it a crime to knowingly give or sell a firearm or ammunition to anyone who is the subject of protection order (Id. § 922(d)(8)).

Disputes over custody of children often arise in domestic violence cases, and protection order courts have been given the authority to issue custody orders. Judges should not look at custody and visitation as unrelated matters in addressing domestic violence cases (Task Force on Racial and Gender Bias, 1992). Resolving custody issues often is as critical as a stay-away order, since disputes over custody frequently provide the opportunity for more violence (Id.). Virtually all states now allow courts to award temporary custody in protection order hearings (Klein & Orloff, 1993; National Council, 1994).

To aid the court in determining child custody, states have begun to set forth standards that should be used in domestic violence cases. The most important trend that has emerged is a presumption against awarding custody to a batterer/parent. In 1990, both houses of Congress passed House Concurrent Resolution 172 which recommended that when deciding any custody case, if there is credible evidence that one spouse abused the other spouse, then there should be a presumption against awarding the abusive spouse custody. The Model Code supports and expands this approach by stating that when the court determines that there was an incident of domestic violence, there is a rebuttable presumption against awarding the batterer sole or joint custody (National Council, § 401, 1994). The Model Code also states that the safety and well-being of the children and the victim should be considered, as well as the history of the batterer's violence (Id. § 402). It is encouraging that courts in many states are looking not only at the child's best interest, but also at the safety of the victim.

The emphasis on a presumption against custody award to batterers is based on data which shows that there is a high correlation between spousal abuse and physical, psychological and emotional trauma to children (National Woman Abuse Prevention Project, 1989). A study by the Boston Children's Hospital abuse program found that 70% of the children in their program who were severely abused had mothers who were also battered (Holmes, 1988). It has been found that many children are injured by their fathers, inadvertently, while the father is throwing furniture or other objects while abusing the mother (Roy, 1988). Younger children are frequently seriously injured, especially when the mother is holding the child to protect him, and the batterer continues to abuse the mother without thinking of the child's safety (Id.).

Providing for safe visitation is also very important in resolving domestic violence situations. Most states grant courts the authority to include a temporary visitation provision in the protection order. It is essential that courts set a very specific visitation plan in each domestic violence case, in order to prevent future conflicts and violence. The National Council of Juvenile and Family Court Judges suggest strongly that courts should consider carefully the violent conduct when issuing a visitation order in a domestic violence case (National Council, 1994). Since there are risks posed to the children by exposing them to a batterer, some states are now requiring courts to order supervised or restricted visitation if it appears that more lenient visitation rights would pose a threat to the children or the abused parent.

The Model Code and many state statutes emphasize the safety and well-being of the abused parent and the children above all other criteria (National Council, § 402, 1994). It also suggests conditions the court can mandate in a visitation order (National Council, § 405, 1994). Some examples include the court arranging for the exchange of the child to be done in a protected setting, ordering that a third party pick up and drop off the child, ordering supervised visitation, ordering the batterer to complete a domestic violence intervention program, and ordering the batterer to refrain from consuming drugs or alcohol during the time spent with the children, and 24 hours prior to the children's arrival (Id.). In addition, overnight visits can be prohibited and a bond can be ordered to ensure the return of the child. The Model Code also suggests that the court have the authority to impose any other condition that would ensure the safety of the child and the abused parent (Id.).

To ensure the child's physical and emotional well-being, supervised visitation is often ordered by the court. However, this places a burden on the parties and the court to develop a mechanism for visitation that will be supervised by a qualified and acceptable third party (Torterella, 1996). Finding a neutral third party is a very difficult task, and requires some cooperation on the part of both parties, which can be dangerous. In most jurisdictions there is no system available to provide professional supervision, so the parties will need to work together to arrange for the visitation. This could cause further conflict, which can undermine the effectiveness of the protection order.

A possible remedy to this problem is to have community based supervised visitation centers (Id.). These centers could provide a variety of services, such as: exchange supervision, telephone monitoring, an observer who remains with the parent and child constantly during visitation or spot checks during the visitation. As of 1995, there were approximately one hundred visitation centers in the country, but they are having trouble remaining open because of the lack of funding (Straus, 1995). The 1995 federal Crime Bill grants the Attorney General the power to allocate funds to local governments so they can set up visitation centers for children who are at risk because of sexual abuse, domestic violence, mental illness, substance abuse of parental kidnaping (42 U.S.C. § 13751(a)(2)(J) (1995)), but many states have not taken advantage of these allocations (Torterella, 1995).

NEGATIVE TRENDS

There are several actions that some jurisdictions permit that can be extremely detrimental to victims of domestic violence and are contrary to the recommendations of legal and judicial domestic violence experts. Mutual protection orders are an example of how courts can sabotage the purposes of domestic violence statutes. A mutual protection order is a protection order that is issued by a court against both the abused petitioner and the abusive respondent without a prior written complaint having been filed against the petitioner or a judicial finding that the petitioner has committed any criminal act. Such orders often provide that both parties shall refrain from abusive behavior and stay away from each other. Entering a mutual protection order sanctions the abusive person's behavior by sending the message that the abused person is partly to blame for the violence and unjustifiably punishes the victim against whom there has not been any evidence or findings of wrongdoing. Mutual protection orders are virtually unenforceable since police cannot discern who was the true abuse victim.

Mutual protection orders also violate the petitioner's right to due process because they are issued without proper notice, such as a separate petition or complaint. The many problems associated with mutual protection orders has led many jurisdictions to bar issuance of a mutual protection order unless each party files a petition (see, e.g., Fla. Stat. Ann. § 741.302(h)(1), (1992); N.Y. Fam. Ct. Act § 841, (1994)). Other states require the court to provide written findings of fact that each party has committed acts of domestic violence when issuing a mutual protection order (see, e.g., N.D. Cent. Code § 14-07.1-02.5, (1993)). In general, most jurisdictions are moving away from the issuance of mutual protection orders.

The Violence Against Women Act ("VAWA") (18 U.S.C. § 2265), a federal law, is designed to discourage judges from issuing mutual orders against domestic violence victims who have not committed acts of abuse or who acted in self defense by making such orders unenforceable across state lines. Under VAWA, protection orders will only be enforced against both parties if a separate complaint or counter petition was filed seeking a protection order, and the court made findings that both parties committed acts of domestic violence (Id.). Additionally, jurisdictions that allow mutual protection orders to be issued do not qualify to receive VAWA funding.

Mediation is also a procedure that is detrimental to victims of domestic violence. Mediation is not an effective way to resolve a domestic violence case because there can be no equal bargaining power among the parties when domestic violence exists in the relationship. Mediation is an alternate dispute method that is supposed to allow the parties to work through their dispute together and devise their own solution. If one party has been a victim of violence and control, the entire process will be dominated by the abuser, defeating the purpose of mediation. Research has shown that during mediation abused women are intimidated by their batterers and are less likely to assert their interests or those of their children because of the fear of future harm and retaliation (Hart, 1990). The American Psychological Association states that "use of mediation is usually not appropriate when family violence is an issue" (APA, 1996). The Model Code strongly recommends that courts not have the authority to order parties into mediation to resolve issues in domestic violence cases (National Council, § 311, 1994). In addition to prohibiting mediation in protection order cases, the Model Code urges that mediation also be prohibited in all divorce and custody proceedings when there is credible evidence of domestic violence (Model Code § 407, 1994; Goolkasian, 1986).

ENFORCEMENT OF PROTECTION ORDERS

Enforcing protection orders is a key element in protecting victims of domestic violence. Without effective enforcement, the entire process of obtaining a protection order can be undermined. When victims are given a false sense of security about the effect of their protection orders, it may increase their danger (Finn and Colson, 1990). A study by the National Institute of Justice stated that for enforcement to be effective, victims need to report violations, courts need to monitor cases, and most importantly, the police, prosecutors and courts should punish offenders so that they will take the order seriously (Id.).

In the past, civil protection orders were primarily enforced by conducting a contempt hearing for any alleged violation. Today, in large part because of VAWA, violation of a protection order is a crime that can be prosecuted in criminal court in most every jurisdiction. However, the petitioner continues to be able to choose to enforce her order through contempt, either civil or criminal (Klein & Orloff, 1993).

In a civil contempt case, the court is seeking to force the respondent to comply with specific protection order terms in the future. Typically a person is held in civil contempt for acts such as failure to pay child support, failure to turn over property, or failure to vacate a family home (Klein & Orloff, 1993). As a contempt sanction, an abuser might be ordered to be incarcerated until such time as he vacates the family home or pays the money due to the petitioner.

Criminal contempt is used to punish a person for a past violation of a protection order (Klein & Orloff, 1993). A person does not have to engage in an action that is considered a separate new crime to be held in criminal contempt of a protection order. A violation of a protection order in any way, such as violating the stay-away provision, may be grounds for criminal contempt. In *State ex rel. Delisser v. Hardy* (1988), a defendant was held in criminal contempt for violating a restraining order upon finding that the defendant entered a multi-unit apartment house, and slipped a note under the petitioner's door. The court held that he did not need to threaten the petitioner directly to come within the meaning of the protection order.

To establish criminal contempt, it must be proved beyond a reasonable doubt that the defendant violated the protection order (*State v. Lipcamon*, 1992; *Vito v. Vito*, 1988). Meeting this burden may sometimes be accomplished simply by the testimony of the petitioner. In *People v. Blackwood* (1985), the court held that the petitioner's uncorroborated testimony that the defendant had threatened her in violation of the protection order was enough to meet the beyond a reasonable doubt standard. The abuse victim's chances of success in the contempt action increase when she provides evidence from corroborating witnesses.

When there has been more than one violation of a protection order, the victim may bring multiple contempt actions. The court may consolidate the violations into a single proceeding; however, each contemptuous act may be punished separately and an individual sentence imposed of up to six months for each. It is important that each individual act is recognized and punished, since each offense affects and injures the victim. This clearly demonstrates to the abusive person that each and every violation has consequences. Many jurisdictions, such as Florida, New Mexico and Louisiana, do not grant the defendant the right to a jury trial when multiple contempt charges are tried together. A recent United States Supreme Court confirmed that when multiple sentences of less than 6 months were aggregated the defendant does not have a right to a jury trial (*Lewis v. United States*, 1996).

Double jeopardy is another constitutional issue that may arise when there is a criminal contempt case. Double jeopardy does not prevent a victim from seeking a protection order based on a specific act that has been criminally prosecuted, but a criminal prosecution may, in some limited cases, be barred because the victim brought a criminal contempt action based on the same act.

In 1993, the Supreme Court decided *United States v. Dixon* (1993), the Court's first ruling on domestic violence. The Supreme Court held that a battered woman would not be barred from enforcing a protection order through a criminal contempt proceeding while the state prosecutes the batterer in a criminal action for the crime, so long as the contempt proceeding and criminal prosecution each require proof of additional elements under the *Blockburger* "same elements" test. The *Blockburger* test is whether each offense requires proof of a fact that the other offense does not (*Blockburger v. United States*, 1932).

In order to prevent double jeopardy from attaching, the petitioner's counsel, petitioner's advocate or the court should communicate with the prosecutor's office to ensure that they are not basing the two actions on the same elements. The decision in *Dixon* allows battered women to enforce their protection orders by pursuing criminal contempt, through which victims may obtain more immediate relief, while also allowing the state to prosecute the offender and protect societal interests.

Another key element to enforcing protection orders and protecting victim's of domestic abuse is the interstate recognition and enforcement of protection orders. Many victims of domestic violence are forced to flee their home state in an effort to stop the abuse that they have been enduring. If the new state does not recognize and enforce the protection order that was issued by another state, victims forced to flee the state that issued the protection order would lose the benefit of that order's protection. The new state may not have jurisdiction to issue another protection order if the abuse occurred in a different state. There may also be other problems such as additional filing fees, inconsistent laws, lack of access to legal services, or difficulty in serving an out-of-state resident.

To address these problems, the Violence Against Women Act mandates interstate enforcement of protection orders. VAWA states that full faith and credit must be given to other states' permanent or *ex parte* temporary protection orders as long as the due process requirements were met in the issuing state (18 U.S.C.A. § 2265). In order to satisfy these requirements, the issuing state must have had personal and subject matter jurisdiction to issue a protection order against the respondent. This essentially means that the court that issued the protection order must have had personal jurisdiction over the parties and subject matter jurisdiction over the controversy. A state can have subject matter jurisdiction either because some act of domestic violence occurred there or, in some states, because the abused victim is present in the state and needs protection.

In addition, the respondent must have had reasonable notice and an opportunity to have been heard. If these due process requirements are satisfied, the protection order must be enforced in the new state, even if, under the second state's laws, the victim could not have qualified for a protection order, or if the relief contained in the protection order would not have been available in the enforcing state. VAWA states that qualified protection orders will be enforced in each and every state as if it were an order of the enforcing state (18 U.S.C.A. § 2265(a)).

Under VAWA, the victim may enforce a protection order issued in another state by any means available. The victim should be able to call the police in the new state to have the abuser arrested for a criminal violation of the protection order. The victim may also file a contempt enforcement action in the new jurisdiction. In addition, the victim should be able to register the protection order in the new jurisdiction. VAWA does not require registration of the foreign protection order in the new state, however, registration may make the foreign protection order more easily enforceable or make the victim feel more secure. The purpose of full faith and credit provisions of VAWA is to allow victims to move between states without the additional burden of petitioning for a new order or registering the foreign protection order. Victims should be protected by their original protection order at all times and in all jurisdictions within the United States.

The Violence Against Women Act has also created two federal crimes for domestic violence. Interstate domestic violence is now a federal offense under § 2261 of the VAWA. This federal law states that it is a federal crime to cross a state line with the intent of injuring a spouse or intimate, if that action actually causes bodily injury. In addition, it is also a federal crime to force or trick a spouse or intimate to cross a state line if an intentional injury results (18 U.S.C.A. § 2261).

Secondly, VAWA also makes it a federal crime when a person crosses a state line with the intent of violating a protection order, and the order is actually violated. To prove this crime, it is sufficient to produce evidence of a history of violence and the timing of the travel. The prosecutor does not have to prove the defendant's specific intent to violate the order (18 U.S.C.A. § 2262). These two actions offer very significant additional protection to women who have fled their home state because of domestic violence.

Under Title III of VAWA, a victim of "a crime of violence motivated by gender" can also seek a civil rights torts remedy. Any person who commits a crime of gender motivated violence shall be liable to the injured party for compensatory and punitive damages, injunctive and declaratory relief, and any other relief that is deemed appropriate by the court (42 U.S.C.A. § 13981). The term "crime of violence" is defined as any act that is considered a felony, against a person or property, and any act that would be considered a felony but for the relationship of the parties (Id.). The victim must also prove that the act committed was motivated by gender (Id.). This relief may be sought against the batterer, in state or federal court., regardless of whether criminal charges were ever brought against him (Id.).

There have been several unsuccessful constitutional challenges raised to the VAWA civil rights remedy. In Connecticut, a wife sought damages based on the civil rights provision of VAWA, and the husband filed a motion to dismiss on grounds that the provision was unconstitutional (*Doe v. Doe*, 1996). Congress enacted the VAWA under the Commerce Clause of the Constitution, which grants Congress the power to regulate anything that affects interstate commerce. The United States District Court of Connecticut found the VAWA civil rights remedy constitutional holding that gender based crimes affect interstate commerce by restricting the movement of victims, limiting the victim's opportunity to engage in interstate business or being employed in interstate business. Essentially, gender motivated crimes decrease national productivity, because abused women cannot contribute fully to the work force, creating a substantial adverse affect on interstate commerce (Id.).

Confidentiality is also an important aspect of protecting victims of domestic violence. Some women need to be able to live and work at a location unknown to their abusers. For these victims, keeping information confidential that could be used to locate them is essential. VAWA includes a provision that requires the United States Post Office to promulgate rules to ensure the confidentiality of the addresses of a victims of domestic violence and domestic violence shelters (42 U.S.C.A. § 13951). A victim needs only to present a valid protection order to an official at the Post Office in order to have them withhold her address and forwarding information from distribution. For a shelter to seek protection, they must show proof to the Post Office that they are a state authorized shelter (Id.).

CONCLUSION

The American judicial system is improving the accessibility and efficiency of the legal protection available to victims of domestic violence. The civil domestic violence laws are helping to empower victims, by providing the protection they need to leave their abusers. Battered women are now able to not only seek an order that prohibits the abuser from contacting the victim, but may also receive monetary relief, child custody, property rights, and any other relief that is essential in ending the violent relationship.

Most jurisdictions today are also beginning to provide protection before the abuse escalates into an even more dangerous and violent pattern, by allowing a victim to seek a civil protection order based on evidence of harassment, stalking and emotional abuse. All states authorize, and a growing number of judges are beginning to be willing to issue, protection orders even if the parties still reside together. These orders play an essential role in curbing domestic violence, since they allow the courts to intervene in violent relationships at an early stage, before the violence escalates and becomes more dangerous. It is important that these innovative and positive trends continue to be demanded and developed by judges, legislators, advocates and victims as we learn more about this tremendously important and devastating societal problem.

REFERENCES

American Psychological Association (1996). *Violence and the Family: Report of the American Psychological Association's Presidential Task Force on Violence and the Family.* Washington DC.

Finn, Peter and Sarah Colson (1990). *Civil Protection Orders: Legislation, Current Court Practice, and Enforcement.* Washington DC: National Institute of Justice.

Follingstad, Diane R. (1990). The Role of Emotional Abuse in Physically Abusive Relationships. *Journal of Family Violence*, 5, 107.

Ganley, Anne L. (1992) Domestic Violence: The What, Why and Who as Relevant to Civil Court Cases. *Domestic Violence in Civil Court Cases: A National Model for Judicial Education.* Jacqueline A. Agtuca et al. eds.

Goolkasian, Gail A. (1986). *Confronting Domestic Violence: The Role of Criminal Court Judges.* Washington DC: U.S. Department of Justice.

Hart, Barbara (1992). State Codes on Domestic Violence: Analysis, Commentary, and Recommendations. *Juvenile and Family Court J. 43*, 58.

Holmes, William M. (1988). *Police Response to Domestic Violence: Final Report for Bureau of Justice Statistics.* Washington DC: US Department of Justice. p. 16.

Klein, Catherine F. and Leslye E. Orloff (1993). Providing Legal Protection for Battered Women: An Analysis of State Statutes and Case Law. *Hofstra Law Review, 21*, 801.

Morrell, Lisa (1984). Violence in Premarital Relationships. *Response, 7*, 17.

National Council of Juvenile and Family Court Judges (1994). *Model Code on Domestic and Family Violence.*

_____ (1990). Family Violence Project, Family Violence: Improving Court Practice, Recommendations from the National Council of Juvenile and Family Court Judges. *Juvenile and Family Court J. 41*, 17.

National Institute of Justice (1993). *Project to Develop a Model Anti-Stalking Code for States.* Washington DC: National Institute of Justice.

National Woman Abuse Prevention Project (1989). *Understanding Domestic Violence*: Fact Sheets 3.

O'Keefe, Nona K. et al. (1986). Teen Dating Violence. *Social Work,* p. 465-466.

Rouse, Linda P. (1988). Abuse in Intimate Relationships: A Comparison of Married and Dating College Students. *J. of Interpersonal Violence 3*, 414-423.

Strauss, Robert A. (1995). Supervised Visitation and Family Violence. *Family Law Quarterly 29*, 229.

Task Force on Racial and Ethnic Bias and Task Force on Gender Bias in the Courts. (1992). *District of Columbia Courts, Final Report.* Washington DC.

Torterella, Margaret (1996). When Supervised Visitation is in the Best Interests of the Child. *Family Law Quarterly 30*, 199.

Walker, Lenore E. (1984). *Eliminating Sexism to End Battering Relationships.* Vol 2.

CASES CITED

Blockburger v. United States, 264 U.S. 299 (1932).

Caldwell v. Coppola, 268 Cal. Rep. 453 (Cal.Ct.App. 1990).

Doe v. Doe, 929 F.Supp. 608 (USDC Conn. 1996).

Diehl v. Drummond, 2 Pa.D. & C.4th 376 (C.P. 1989).

In re Marriage of Blitstein, 569 N.E.2d 1357 (Ill.App.Ct. 1991).

Lewis v. United States, 116 S. Ct. 2163 (1996).

Matter of Baker, 494 N.W.2d 282 (Minn.1992).

Parkhurst v. Parkhurst, 793 S.W.2d 634 (Mo.Ct.App. 1990).

People v. Blackwood, 476 N.E.2d 742 (Ill.App.Ct. 1985).

Pierson v. Pierson, 555 NYS.2d 227 (Fam.Ct. 1990).

Powell v. Powell, 547 A.2d 973 (D.C. 1988).

Rayan v. Dykeman, 274 Cal. Reptr. 672 (Ct.App. 1990).

Sielski v. Sielski, 604 A.2d 206 (N.J.Super.Ct.Ch.Div. 1992).

State ex.rel. Delisser v. Hardy, 749 P.2d 1207 (Or.Ct.Àpp. 1988).

State v. Lipcamon, 483 N.W.2d 605 (Iowa 1992).

State v. Wiltse, 386 N.W.2d 315 (Minn.App. 1986).

Stuckey v. Stuckey, 768 P.2d 694 (Colo.1989).

United States v. Dixon and United States v. Foster, 113 S.Ct. 2849 (1993).

Vito v. Vito, 551 A.2d 573 (Pa.Super.Ct. 1988).

Wagner v. Wagner, 15 Pa.D. & C.3d 148 (C.P. 1980).

STATUTES CITED

United States Code Annotated (Supp. 1995). 18: §§ 2261; 2262; 2265.

United States Code (Supp. 1995) 18 § 922; 42: §§ 13751; 13951; 13981.

Alabama Code § 30-5-2 (Supp. 1993).

Connecticut General Statutes Annotated § 46(b)-14 (West Supp. 1993).

Delaware Code Annotated § 10:945-949 (1993).

District of Columbia Code Annotated § 16-1005 (1981).

Georgia Code Annotated § 19-13-1-4 (Supp. 1993).
Florida Statutes Annotated § 741.302 (West Supp. 1993).
Hawaii Revised Statutes § 586-1-4 (Supp. 1992).
Indiana Code Annotated § 34-4-5 (1986 & Supp. 1993).
Immigration and Nationality Act, 8 U.S.C. § 1186 (Supp. IV 1994).
Louisiana Revised Statutes Annotated § 46:2132-2135 (Supp. 1992).
New Hampshire Revised Statutes Annotated § 173 (Supp. 1993).
New Jersey Statutes Annotated §§ 2c:25-18-19; 25-29 (West Supp. 1993).
New Mexico Statutes Annotated § 40-13-2 (Michie Supp. 1993).
New York Family Court Act Law §§ 812; 821; 842 (Mc Kinney Supp. 1994).
Nevada Revised Statutes Annotated § 33.018 (Michie 1996).
North Dakota Cent. Code § 14.07.1 (Supp. 1993).
Oklahoma Statutes Annotated § 22:60.1 (Supp. 1993).
Pennsylvania Cons. Statutes Annotated § 23:6102-6108 (1983).
Puerto Rico Laws Annotated, § 8:664 (1990).
Rhode Island General Laws § § 8-8.1-1; 15-15-1; 11-59-2 (Supp. 1993).
Washington Revised Code Annotated § 26.50 (1993).
West Virginia Code § 48-2A-2 (West 1993).
Wyoming Statutes § 35-21-102, 105 (Supp. 1993).
Vermont Statutes Annotated § 1104 (1992).

Police Handling
of Domestic Violence Calls:
An Overview and Further Investigation

Lynette Feder

SUMMARY. This study compares the rates and correlates associated with an arrest response when police respond to domestic assault calls in one jurisdiction at one point in time through two different methodological approaches–police self-report and case record analysis. While police self-reported a high likelihood to arrest (approximately a 60% rate of arrest), police reports indicated a much lower rate of arrest (20%). However, the two methodologies showed greater similarities in terms of correlates associated with this arrest response. Specifically, both indicated the predominance of situational factors over officer, offender or victim characteristics. *[Article copies available for a fee from The Haworth Document Delivery Service: 1-800-342-9678. E-mail address: getinfo@haworthpressinc. com]*

LITERATURE REVIEW

Wife assault has a long history in western civilization (Davidson, 1977). In this country, most states disallowed wifebeating by the late nineteenth century (Taub, 1983). Still, even as courts rejected this right, they held, ". . . if no permanent injury has been inflicted, nor malice, cruelty or dangerous violence shown by the husband, it is better to draw the curtain, shut out the

---

Lynette Feder, PhD, Associate Professor, Department of Criminal Justice, Florida Atlantic University, 777 West Glades Road, Boca Raton, FL 33431.

[Haworth co-indexing entry note]: "Police Handling of Domestic Violence Calls: An Overview and Further Investigation." Feder, Lynette. Co-published simultaneously in *Women & Criminal Justice* (The Haworth Press, Inc.) Vol. 10, No. 2, 1999, pp. 49-68; and: *Women and Domestic Violence: An Interdisciplinary Approach* (ed: Lynette Feder) The Haworth Press, Inc., 1999, pp. 49-68. Single or multiple copies of this article are available for a fee from The Haworth Document Delivery Service [1-800-342-9678, 9:00 a.m. - 5:00 p.m. (EST). E-mail address: getinfo@haworthpressinc.com].

public gaze, and leave the parties to forget and forgive" [*State v. Oliver*, 70 N.C. 60, 61-62, (1873)]. Thus, although wifebeating was illegal in most states by the late 1800s, few incidents resulted in arrest or prosecution of the offender.

This approach to domestic violence remained in place until the 1960s when police departments across the nation were called upon to become more actively involved in domestic violence (Breci, 1989; Friedman & Shulman, 1990). The request originally took the form of asking police to act as mediators or counselors. Specifically, the Department of Justice provided funds to police departments nationwide to train law enforcement officers on counseling and mediation techniques when handling domestic violence calls (Sherman, 1988). It was thought that this approach would reduce the risk of violence to the police officer and the victim.

By the 1970s, however, this method fell in disfavor. Many criticized the mediation approach as being too soft on offenders (Sherman, 1988; Friedman & Shulman, 1990). At the same time, advocates for battered women were asserting that women victims of domestic assault received less protection from the police than their non-domestic assault counterpart. Research from this time period supported their assertion. For instance, Black's critical study observed all police-citizen encounters in three cities. His findings indicated that the victim-offender relationship was more important in accounting for variation in police likelihood to arrest than the severity of crime (Black, 1978). Data from another large police observational study conducted in several cities in 1977 concluded that, while police were as likely to arrest domestic as non-domestic violence offenders, legal and evidentiary variables (such as severity of offense and victim's cooperation) would argue for a higher rate of arrest in domestic assault cases. Therefore, the police were practicing a policy of underenforcement when responding to domestic assault calls (Oppenlander, 1982).

This pattern of underenforcement continued. Domestic violence was rarely treated as a crime except in the most brutal cases. Otherwise, police engaged in a policy of underenforcement reflecting their ambivalence about this issue. There were many reasons given as to why police were reluctant to arrest when responding to domestic assault calls. Many pointed to the police officers' belief that violence in the family was a private not public matter (Buzawa & Buzawa, 1985; Mederer & Gelles, 1989). The system of rewards practiced in police departments also explained this pattern of underenforcement (Buzawa & Buzawa, 1985). Another factor noted frequently was the police officers' belief that the victim would have a change of heart leading to unsuccessful prosecution of the offender (Buzawa, 1982; Sherman, 1988). And, too, there was the worry that an arrest would lead to greater risk of injury to the victim (Buzawa & Austin, 1985; Sherman, 1988).

Perhaps the most serious impediment to an arrest response was due to structural considerations–constraints imposed upon the police legally. Unlike the law of felony arrest, the law of misdemeanor arrest allowed police to take a defendant into custody only when the officer had witnessed the incident. Lacking this, the officer needed to first obtain an arrest warrant. Since most domestic violence incidents were (and are) treated as misdemeanors, this necessarily meant that for most domestic violence calls police did not have legal authority to make an immediate arrest (Buzawa, 1982; Sherman, 1988). Added to this quagmire, police also had to worry about civil liability if the victim later recanted her testimony (Buzawa & Buzawa, 1985).

In the 1970s, a plethora of factors coalesced around this issue and changed the way society and the police viewed, and handled, cases of wife beating. First, there was the women's movement which identified domestic violence as a major issue. They demanded that police take a law enforcement stand when responding to these calls (Greenblat, 1965). Litigation also led police to respond more proactively when dealing with domestic assault calls. During this time, several important lawsuits were brought against large police departments alleging denial of equal protection under the law when the police failed to respond vigorously to assaults perpetrated upon women by husbands and boyfriends (*Bruno v. Codd*, 1976; *Scott v. Hurt*, 1976; *Thomas v. Los Angeles*, 1979). Though police responded to these lawsuits by agreeing to treat domestic assault as a crime in the future, many still did not see any significant changes in law enforcement policies. A few years later, the courts went even further. In *Thurman v. City of Torrington* (1984), the police were held liable for the injuries a battered wife sustained when the police failed to respond seriously to her requests for help.

Finally, the results from a large research study helped change the police perspective on the handling of such calls. In 1981, the Minneapolis Police Department participated in an experiment which assessed the effectiveness of three responses–mediate, separate, or arrest–in preventing future domestic assault. The Minneapolis Experiment indicated that arrest led to significantly lower rates of recidivism whether measured through official arrest data or victim reports. The researchers concluded that arrest should be the response of choice by the police (Sherman & Berk, 1984).

Even though replication of this experiment has not consistently achieved similar results (Dunford, Huizinga & Delbert, 1990; Hirschel, Hutchinson & Dean, 1992), research indicates that this experiment has been significant in changing the policies of police departments nationwide (Sherman & Cohn, 1989). Due to the changes described above, among others, many police departments began adopting pro-arrest policies in response to misdemeanor domestic assault (Steinman, 1990).

State legislatures also began to directly address the problem of domestic violence. First they passed legislation allowing police to make warrantless probable cause arrests for misdemeanor domestic assaults whether or not the crime occurred in their presence. Additional legislation protecting police from civil liability when handling these calls was also important since police no longer had to be concerned with a wrongful arrest suit where the victim recanted her allegation. But even as obstacles to arresting the misdemeanor domestic violence offender were removed, there remained a widely held belief that police were still underenforcing the law (Oppenlander, 1982). Once again, the legislators responded. This time they wrote statutes mandating or presuming an arrest response when police answered domestic assault calls.

With the advent of these new legislative statutes and departmental policies requiring police to adopt a law enforcement approach when responding to domestic violence, researchers followed-up with investigations on the impact of these laws and policies on police behavior (Blount, Yegedis & Maheux, 1992; Buzawa, 1982; Ferraro, 1989). Research entered a new phase of inquiry focusing on whether the behavior of police personnel could be changed by mandating a particular policy (Balos and Trotzky, 1988; Lawrenz, Lembo & Shade, 1988; Ferraro, 1989). Studies looking to measure the impact of these laws on police response either surveyed police (see Walter, 1981; Dolon, Hendricks & Meagher, 1986; Belknap & McCall, 1994; Belknap, 1995) or observed them in their handling of domestic assault calls (for example Oppenlander, 1982; Worden & Pollitz, 1984; Ferraro, 1989). Research also utilized written case records to establish police handling of these cases (see Berk & Loseke, 1980-81; Bell, 1985; Lawrenz et al., 1988), or surveyed known victims about their perceptions of police response (see for instance, Brown, 1984; Gondolf & McFerron, 1989; Buzawa and Austin, 1993).

These studies indicated that the legislative intent was meeting with only limited success in changing the behavior of police personnel. This finding held regardless of the methodology used. Even where there was extensive injury to the victim, studies indicated a rate of arrest that rarely fell outside the 11% to 22% range (see for instance Brown, 1984; Erez, 1986; Dutton, 1987). Not surprisingly, the result was low rates of victim satisfaction with police (Bowker, 1982; Kennedy & Homant, 1983; Balos & Trotzky, 1988).

Later, researchers began investigating the correlates associated with police likelihood to arrest. Factors associated with an arrest outcome when responding to domestic violence can be organized into four groupings: police, offender, victim and situational characteristics. In investigating police officer characteristics, researchers found that training was positively associated (Buzawa, 1982; Breci & Simons, 1987; Buzawa, 1988), while attitudes towards women's roles (that is, belief in traditional sex roles) was negatively associated (Saunders and Size, 1986; Stith, 1990; Feder, 1997) with police likelihood to arrest when responding to a domestic assault call. The result on the officer's standing on the Straus Conflict Tactics Scale (measuring the amount of verbal and physical aggression used at home) (Stith, 1990; Feder, 1997) was not consistently found to relate to an arrest response. Similarly, research results indicated contradictory findings regarding the officer's age (Buzawa, 1982; Buzawa, 1988; Stith, 1990), gender (Homant & Kennedy, 1985; Blount et al., 1992) and time on force (Blount et al., 1992; Feder, 1997) and likelihood to arrest.

In investigating offender factors, researchers generally found that prior assaultive behavior (Smith & Klein, 1984; Waaland & Keeley, 1985; Gondolf & McFerron, 1989), use of drugs or alcohol (Smith & Klein, 1984; Worden & Pollitz, 1984; Berk, Fenstermaker & Newton, 1988), and a disrespectful demeanor towards police (Smith & Klein, 1984; Worden & Pollitz, 1984; Dolon et al., 1986) were all positively correlated with arrest likelihood. Contradictory results were found on the impact of the offender's gender on an arrest outcome (Berk & Loseke, 1980-81; Smith & Visher, 1981). Victim's calling for help (as opposed to someone other than the victim calling for help) was negatively associated with an arrest outcome (Berk & Loseke, 1980-81; Berk et al., 1988). And while many assume that police are less likely to arrest where the victim is drinking or drunk, only one study could be found directly testing this assumption (Waaland & Keeley, 1985). Finally, there are mixed findings as to the significance of the couple's marital status (Berk & Loseke, 1980-81; Erez, 1986; Berk et al., 1988) and race (Smith & Klein, 1984; Worden & Pollitz, 1984; Berk et al., 1988) on police officers' likelihood to arrest.

By far, situational characteristics have been found to have the largest and most consistent effect on police likelihood to arrest when responding to domestic violence. For instance, victim injury is consistently associated with a higher likelihood of arrest (Ferraro, 1989; Gondolf & McFerron, 1989; Buzawa & Austin, 1993).[1] Victim's preference for an arrest or a willingness to sign a complaint has also been found to consistently relate to the likelihood of an arrest response (Berk & Loseke, 1980-81; Dolon et al., 1986).[2] And finally, offender's presence has been found to consistently relate to an arrest outcome (Berk & Loseke, 1980-81; Feder, 1996).

Each of the methods used in the research studies above has its inevitable shortcomings (Dutton, 1988). For instance, survey research may be contaminated by the respondent's desire to answer in a socially desirable manner. On the other hand, case records may be nothing more than after the fact reconstructions of incidents to justify police decisions. Finally, observational research runs the risk of changing what is being observed. This is precisely the reason why experts recommend triangulation, or the use of multiple methods, when assessing a phenomenon (Babbie, 1993).

This study, therefore, seeks to do exactly that by investigating police officers' likelihood to arrest when responding to a domestic assault incident, along with the correlates associated with the decision to arrest, by using a multiple method approach in one jurisdiction at one point in time. Police officers' self-reported likelihood to arrest, and the correlates associated with this decision, will be compared to rates and correlates of arrest according to police case records. This analysis will therefore provide information on the rates and correlates of arrest in one pro-arrest jurisdiction, along with a comparison of research results using two methodologies–police surveys and case record analysis–to study an arrest decision.

RESEARCH METHODOLOGY

The study was conducted out of Palm Beach Sheriff's Office–one of the largest police agencies in south Florida. The department has achieved recognition for its professionalism and has gone on record supporting a pro-arrest law enforcement stand in the handling of domestic assault. In fact, this agency had a written pro-arrest departmental policy long before the new legislation was implemented. Beyond the policy, though, was departmental action designed to let all officers know that an arrest was the preferred outcome when dealing with a domestic call. Specifically, officers were well aware that they could be suspended for failing to comply with this policy. (One officer had been suspended shortly before the survey and another was suspended shortly following survey completion.)

In the summer of 1992, the researcher received approval to hand out a two-page anonymous survey questionnaire to all police officers on all shifts attending roll call. To maximize the possibility of obtaining all officers' responses, each shift's roll call was attended twice within a two and one-half week interval. The researcher received complete cooperation from all but one officer who refused to answer the survey. Therefore, of a total of 412 officers, 297 officers (72%) were surveyed. The remaining 115 officers were either on vacation during the survey period or they did not regularly attend roll call. The latter speaks to those officers who were not patrol officers assigned to this jurisdiction (e.g., patrol officers contracted out to other districts, officers assigned to the Parks or K-9 division, etc.).

One year later the researcher returned and requested all calls for service and the records some of them subsequently generated during the same period that officers had been surveyed one year earlier. It was decided to use the call for service as the starting point for the case record analysis because of research indicating that domestic calls may be handled differently from the time the call is first received by the police (Oppenlander, 1982). Therefore, to circumvent this potential danger, the sampling frame began with all calls for service received by this police department.[3] This method serves as a check against the possibility that a domestic call might be subtly winnowed out at an early point in the process that would then go unrecognized if the research began at a later point in the system. Finally, since domestic assault incidents may be originally classified under many different headings, it was decided to include all incoming calls for service labeled as disturbance, domestic, fight, or assault. For purposes of this research, "domestic" was defined according to Florida law. As such it includes incidents where the victim and offender are or have been married, cohabitating, or romantically involved.

Obviously, the two sources of information are not directly comparable. For instance, while the former uses the officer as the case ($N = 297$), the latter uses calls for service ($N = 627$) and the case records some of them generate ($N = 356$). But beyond that, a method based on surveying police can ask many questions concerning individual officers (for instance, their attitudes towards women's roles, their use of verbal and physical aggression in their own homes, along with their demographics). Alternately, the case record approach will be richer in terms of information on the specific incidents of any given situation. However, while the two may not be directly comparable, and caution needs to be used when interpreting findings, there will be some overlap and each can provide a complement to the other.

Our question concerns the rate of arrest when responding to domestic violence for police in a pro-arrest jurisdiction when using police self-report versus case record research. We next look at the correlates associated with the decision to arrest to see if there are differences between what police say they look at when making this decision and what, in fact, is correlated with the decision to arrest according to case records.

RESEARCH RESULTS

Police Self-Report

The typical police officer from this department is a married middle-aged male who has been a police officer for a little over ten years. The average officer has slightly less than two years of college education though almost 14% ($N = 41$) have a college degree. An additional 6% ($N = 17$) have graduate credits. Furthermore, three-quarters of the force was able to correctly state their department's policy on handling domestic assault calls. Perhaps this high figure reflects the large amount of domestic assault training these officers said they received (approximately 27 hours in the last five years).

In terms of attitudes, these officers' scores on the Attitudes Towards Women's Roles (ATWR) showed a far more flexible view of gender roles than some researchers have assumed (Saunders & Size, 1986). Officers' responses to the Straus Conflict Tactics Scale to assess the amount of verbal and physical force tolerated within their own homes[4] also showed some surprises. While some assume that police officers are more likely to use force at home than those in the general population (Davis, 1981; Walter, 1981), this study found no support for this assertion. Specifically, comparisons of officers' scores on the CTS with other groups indicate that there are similarities in the amount of force officers reported using within their homes (Straus, 1977-78).

Continuing with officers' attitudes, the next series of questions investigated how officers perceived the role of police in domestic violence calls using the Pro-Police Intervention Scale (PPI). In contrast to findings from other studies (Davis, 1981; Lerman, 1982; Balos & Trotzky, 1988), these officers indicated strong support for police intervention when dealing with domestic calls. Most of the officers (79%) believed in the utility of arrest when responding to domestic violence and felt that these calls were a legitimate part of their job as a police officer (89%). Additionally, the majority of officers (60%) supported a mandatory arrest policy when responding to domestic violence.

Though self-report surveys always suffer from respondents' desire to answer in what they perceive as a socially desirable manner, nowhere is this more likely than in the next section: police officers' self-reported response to a variety of domestic assault scenarios (e.g., "A husband slaps his wife around because he was: drunk; she disobeyed him; he was laid off at his job"). As can be seen from Table 1, there was some variation from one scenario to the next in police use of arrest. Officers were least likely to arrest when the husband had just been laid off from his job or he had just learned of his wife's sexual infidelity and were most likely to arrest when the husband was drunk. An additional analysis was conducted (whereby the three non-arrest responses were collapsed into one category and compared to the arrest category) to test whether a widely cited finding—that police were more likely to arrest when the offender was drunk—achieved statistical significance. In line with past findings (Worden & Pollitz, 1984; Berk et al., 1988; Gondolf & McFerron, 1989), results indicated that the police were significantly more likely to arrest when the husband was drunk ($t(253) = -18.83$, $p < .001$). Overall, though police officers were more likely to arrest than not arrest in each of the scenarios, only 41% of the officers (N = 104) indicated that they would arrest in all cases. In contrast, 18% of the officers (N = 46) responded that they would never arrest in any of the scenarios provided. On average, officers reported that they would arrest in a little over four of the seven scenarios.

The next section of the study seeks to understand variation in officers'

TABLE 1. Police Officers' Response (N = 266) to Domestic Assault Scenarios Based on Police Survey*

	Restore Order	Separate	Mediate	Arrest
"A husband slaps his wife around because _____"				
He was drunk	4%	14%	3%	79%
She disobeyed him	10%	9%	25%	56%
He was laid off at his job	11%	7%	29%	52%
She nagged him incessantly	8%	14%	23%	56%
She was drunk	10%	21%	16%	54%
He just learned of her sexual infidelity	8%	19%	21%	52%
She insulted him in front of his friends	10%	13%	20%	58%

* Excludes officers who upgraded one or more of their responses to an arrest (N = 31).

self-reported likelihood to arrest when responding to domestic assault calls using an array of officer demographics, attitudes, training and behavior outside of their job (see Table 2). The Arrest Likelihood Scale (ALS) was defined as the number of times a police officer self-reported an arrest response in each of the seven scenarios and ranged from 0 to 7. Using the ALS as the dependent variable, and excluding those officers who had upgraded their arrest likelihood,[5] the following variables were entered stepwise into the regression equation: demographic variables (officer's gender, marital status, number of years of education completed, and years on the force); attitude towards women's roles (ATWR); training and knowledge of the department's policy on domestic calls; whether they believed in a pro-police intervention (PPI) in domestic calls (that is, they felt that police had a legitimate role to play in domestic calls and that this role could positively impact on the problem); and the amount of violence experienced in their own home (CTS).

Fully 24% of the variation in likelihood to arrest can be explained by the above factors. However, only four variables: Attitudes Toward Women's Roles (ATWR), Knowledge of Department's Policy, belief in a Pro-Police Intervention (PPI) and the number of years the officer had been on the force were significant in accounting for the variation in officers' likelihood to arrest. Of these variables, PPI explained the largest amount of variation in arrest likelihood, followed by Knowledge of Department's Policy, Attitudes

TABLE 2. Factors Associated with Police Likelihood to Arrest Based on Police Survey

Variables	Beta
Attitudes Towards Women's Roles*	.17
Knowledge of Domestic Policy*	.20
Marital Status	.07
Educational Level	−.09
Pro-Police Intervention*	.31
Amount of Domestic Training	.01
Officer Gender	−.03
Use of Physical Force in Home	−.05
Number of Years on Force*	−.12

R Square   .235
F   15.505
Signif F   .000

* Indicates statistical significance at the $p < .05$ probability level.

Towards Women's Roles and officer's years on the force. Specifically, officers who held a pro-police intervention perspective (that is, they thought that domestic calls were very much a part of policing and felt they could impact positively on this problem in their role as a police officer) were more likely to report that they would arrest. Additionally, knowledge of the department's domestic assault policy, as well as viewing women in other than traditional roles, all led to a higher likelihood to arrest. However, the longer an officer had been on the force, the less likely he was to respond with an arrest when answering a domestic assault call. Interestingly, all other officer demographics (including educational level, gender and marital status), in addition to the amount of training they received on handling domestic calls, and their standing on the Conflict Tactics Scale, were not significantly related to their self-reported likelihood to arrest when responding to domestic calls.

Finally, our last section of the survey provided police with one scenario that varied on three factors and then asked the officer how he would handle the call. The first factor investigated was the victim's preference for an arrest outcome (victim wanted an arrest versus victim does not want an arrest). The second looked at the extent of victim injuries (clothes in disarray with a red mark on the woman's face versus woman is cut on her lip and is slightly bleeding from the nose). Finally, the last factor to vary looked at the offender demeanor to police (offender respectful versus offender loud, belligerent and cursing police officer).

ANOVA was used to measure the action the police officer reported he would take when responding to this call for service. (Action was coded as 0 if he would do other than arrest and 1 if he would arrest.) The analyses indicated no significant main effects for victim injury or offender's demeanor towards the police officer in terms of its affect on the likelihood of an arrest response. However, there was a significant main effect for the victim's preference for an arrest outcome (F (1, 286) = 5.69, p = .02), indicating that police were more likely to arrest when the victim requested an arrest ($\bar{x}$ = .799) than when there was no such request ($\bar{x}$ = .690).

Police Case Records

During that seventeen day period, the police received 627 calls for service that were classified as disturbance (n = 133), assault (n = 121), fight (n = 36) or domestic assault (n = 337). Of these calls, 57% (N = 356) involved incidents where the police were dispatched and wrote subsequent reports. While significant differences maintained between those calls for service which received police dispatch (N = 356) and those where police did not attend to the call (N = 271), the analysis finds no support that dispatchers treated incoming domestic assault calls less seriously than other calls. When the three categories of disturbance, assault and fight were collapsed and compared to domestic assaults, police were significantly more likely to be sent out to calls classified by the dispatchers as domestic (χ^2 (1, N = 627) = 12.26, p < .05). Additionally, police were significantly more likely to be dispatched when the victim was female (χ^2 (1, N = 406) = 3.27, p < .05)[6] and when the victim placed the call (χ^2 (1, N = 464) = 3.94, p < .05). This runs contrary to previous research findings that police departments are less responsive to female victims (Smith, 1987) or are less likely to answer calls from victims (Berk & Loseke, 1980-81; Berk et al., 1988).

Of the 337 calls received by dispatchers classified as domestic, an officer was sent to the location in 213 of these cases (63%). Table 3 provides summary information that came from these police records. As can be seen, almost half of the offenders (48%) were not present when police arrived. Of those who were present, the police records noted that they averaged 32.8 years of age with most being white (85%) and male (84%). In only 9% of the cases did the police officer note alcohol or drug use or abuse by the offender. Similarly, only a small percentage of all offenders were noted by police to be belligerent (6%).

The victims averaged 31.4 years of age. Once again, most were white (83%) and female (84%). The police noted alcohol or drug use or abuse in

TABLE 3. Summary Information on Domestic Calls Receiving Follow-Up Police Visits (N = 213) Based on Police Survey

Offender Characteristics:

Age	$\bar{x}$ = 32.8 years	
Race		
White	85%	(98)
Black	15%	(17)
Gender		
Male	84%	(108)
Female	16%	(20)
Alcohol/Drug Use		
No	91%	(116)
Yes	9%	(12)
Belligerent to Officer		
No	94%	(120)
Yes	6%	(8)

Victim Characteristics:

Age	$\bar{x}$ = 31.4 years	
Race		
White	83%	(99)
Black	17%	(20)
Gender		
Male	17%	(21)
Female	84%	(106)
Alcohol/Drug Use		
No	97%	(123)
Yes	3%	(4)
Belligerent to Officer		
No	98%	(125)
Yes	2%	(2)
Victim & Defendant Married		
No	56%	(106)
Yes	44%	(83)

Situational Characteristics:

Offender Present at Scene When Police Arrived	52%	(66)
Violence Level		
None	14%	(25)
Verbal Aggresion	27%	(48)
Threats and/or Property Damage	11%	(19)
Physical Aggression	47%	(83)
Victim Wants Arrest	51%	(55)

TABLE 3 (continued)

Situational Characteristics (continued):

Case Disposition
Nothing	56%	(102)
Separate or Mediate	19%	(34)
Refer	5%	(9)
Arrest	20%	(38)

only 3% of the cases and even fewer victims were noted by police as being belligerent (2%). According to the police records, 44% of the couples were married. Almost half of these calls were reported to involve some level of physical aggression with exactly half resulting in some or great injury to the victim. A slight majority of victims (51%) indicated a preference for an arrest. According to the information provided in the case records, the police arrested in 20% of the cases.

To decipher which of the above variables were significant in predicting an arrest response, the case's disposition was dichotomized into an arrest versus non-arrest response. Using arrest as the dependent variable, offender characteristics (acting belligerent, using drugs or alcohol, race, age and gender), victim characteristics (using drugs or alcohol and victim/offender married) and situational characteristics (level of violence, victim injured, offender present when police arrived, victim preference for an arrest outcome) were regressed on arrest.

As Table 4 indicates, fully 36% of the variance in the police decision to arrest was explained by these variables. However, only three variables were significant in accounting for variance in this outcome. In order of their impact they are offender's presence at the scene when police arrived,[7] victim preference for an arrest outcome and victim injury. All three variables were positively related to the dependent variable. Of interest is what failed to impact upon the arrest decision. All of the offender characteristics (acting belligerent, using drugs or alcohol, race, age and gender) and victim characteristics (using drugs or alcohol and victim/offender married) were not significant in predicting an arrest response. Of the situational characteristics entered, though, only level of violence did not significantly distinguish between those cases where the police responded with an arrest and those where they disposed of the case using other than an arrest response. While at first surprising, it must be remembered that the extent of victim injuries significantly predicted an arrest response. Therefore, police seem to be gauging the outcome of the violence rather than the level of the violence displayed.

TABLE 4. Factors Associated with Police Likelihood to Arrest Based on Police Reports

Variables	Beta
Offender Characteristics:	
Age	.02
Gender	.01
Race	.17
Use Drugs/Alcohol	.12
Belligerent to Police	.18
Victim Characteristcs:	
Use Drugs/Alcohol	−.03
Victim/Offender Married	.02
Situational Characteristics:	
Level of Violence	.06
Victim Injured*	.34
Offender Present*	.40
Victim Wants Arrest*	.31

R Square	.362
F	11.733
Signif F	.000

* Indicates statistical significance at the p < .05 probability level.

CONCLUSION AND DISCUSSION

While these two databases are not directly comparable, there is enough overlap between them to allow for some cautious comparisons. Forty-one percent of the officers (n = 104) said they would arrest in all seven of the domestic assault scenarios presented in the survey. The average rate of arrest for all officers surveyed was 4.166 arrests in the seven situations provided (or a 60% rate of arrest). Therefore, whether we look at number of officers arresting or number of incidents where they would arrest, the police in this jurisdiction self-report a much higher likelihood to arrest than indicated in other studies which relied on police survey (Davis, 1983; Waaland and Keeley, 1985; Buzawa, 1988; Blount et al., 1992).

In comparison, case record analysis (based on police reports) indicates a 20% rate of arrest for domestic assault calls which police responded to during the same period of time that they were being surveyed. Therefore, in one jurisdiction at one period of time we see police self-reporting a higher likelihood to arrest than was being demonstrated in the streets. One could argue that the scenarios provided in the police survey might be more violent and therefore lead to a higher likelihood to arrest than what police were seeing in the streets. However, given the low level of violence portrayed in the scenarios and the fact that 50% of the victims in the police reports were noted as having some or great injury,[8] this explanation seems unlikely.

Where there was overlap between factors investigated, the two methodologies showed greater similarities in terms of the correlates associated with an arrest response than in their rates of arrest. Specifically, victim preference for an arrest response was highly predictive of police taking the defendant into custody in both police self-report and case record analyses. Additionally, the offender acting in a belligerent manner was not significant in predicting an arrest response with either of these methodologies. One of the most important differences between the two methodologies, though, arises in terms of the importance of victim injuries in explaining an arrest decision. While police self-reports failed to find this significantly related to an arrest decision, case record analysis indicated that it was positively associated to an arrest outcome. Possibly this difference was due to the low level of violence portrayed in the scenarios (i.e., she was cut on her upper lip and slightly bleeding from her nose).

While most officer characteristics (e.g., gender, age, marital status, number of years education, training and score on the Straus Conflict Tactics Scale) were not found to be significant, the number of years the officer had been on the force was significantly and negatively related to an arrest decision. In addition, the officer's attitudes towards women's roles, his knowledge of departmental policy on domestic assault and his holding a pro-police intervention position (belief that handling domestic violence was a legitimate part of police work and that he could positively intervene in these cases) positively related to an arrest outcome. Finally, offender characteristics (e.g., offender belligerent, using alcohol/drugs, race, age or gender) were not associated with an arrest response. Neither were victim characteristics (e.g., use of drugs or alcohol and victim/offender married).

Comparing these findings to those from other published studies indicates that the police in this jurisdiction self-report a much higher likelihood to arrest (60%) while demonstrating (through police reports) a somewhat higher likelihood to arrest (20%) than is found elsewhere. The latter finding is still higher than what other comparable case record studies have found. Specifically, other studies have found a 12% (Erez, 1986) or 13% (Bell, 1985) rate of arrest, with one study in a *mandatory* arrest jurisdiction finding as high as a 22% rate of arrest (Balos & Trotzky, 1988).

Possibly, this higher arrest rate in this jurisdiction reflects the officers' view of police as having a legitimate role in domestic calls, one which leads to an effective outcome. In comparison to other studies, the police from this department did not think that domestic violence was a natural part of family life (Davis, 1981; Davis, 1983) and they viewed domestic calls as a legitimate part of police work (Walter, 1981; Belknap, 1995). Not surprisingly, and in contrast to other studies (Lerman, 1982; Jaffe et al., 1986), these officers felt that they could positively intervene in domestic violence calls. Support for this hypothesis can be found in past research which indicates that officers who believe that law enforcement can positively intervene in domestic violence are more likely to arrest when responding to these calls (Blount et al., 1992).

This difference in rates of arrest between this study and others may also signal that, where top administration goes on record in support of an arrest response when answering domestic assault calls, police are more likely to arrest. This interpretation finds support when one compares the rates of arrest for domestic and non-domestic assault calls, controlling for all other legal variables, in this department. Such a comparison indicates that police are twice as likely to arrest when responding to a domestic call than a non-domestic call (20% versus 10% respectively) (Feder, 1998).

In the end, we have two different methodologies which, though they show some differences in findings, show other important similarities. Taken together, the two studies highlight the primacy of situational variables rather than officer, offender or victim characteristics in explaining an arrest decision when police in this one jurisdiction confront a domestic assault call. Of course, without a comparison investigation of correlates associated with an arrest in non-domestic assault calls in this jurisdiction we cannot assume that similar "amounts" of these variables lead equally to an arrest decision in domestic and non-domestic assault calls. Additionally, those officer characteristics which were found to relate to an arrest outcome (e.g., holding a pro-police perspective and knowledge of departmental domestic violence policy) are those which can be impacted upon by the organization. Finally, comparisons between this study's findings and those contained in the literature, again show greater similarity. Still, differences were found and this then tells us the importance of triangulation when conducting research. Specifically, researchers need to address the impact of the methodology on the results obtained.

NOTES

1. Though a summary of the literature indicates that this factor consistently influences the arrest decision, this cannot be taken to mean that the police are using the same standard of injury when deciding to arrest in domestic versus non-domestic assault calls. Such an assumption would have to be tested by comparing the rates and factors associated with these two types of calls. To date, three studies have done this and have come to very different conclusions (see Oppenlander, 1982; Eigenberg, Scarborough & Kappeler, 1997; Feder, 1998).

2. The author is not attaching a value judgement about whether this practice is proper. There are many who would note that police refusal to arrest unless the victim of domestic violence signs the complaint places an unfair hardship upon these women (Jaffe, Wolfe, Telford & Austin, 1986; and Friedman & Shulman, 1990).

3. Whenever a citizen calls for help in this jurisdiction, the call is taken through their Computer Assisted Dispatch System (CADS). Regardless of whether or not an officer is dispatched to the site or subsequently makes a written police report, the CADS unit makes a written record of the call that includes cursory information about the incident.

4. It needs to be noted that there have been valid concerns raised about the Conflict Tactics Scale including that the measure does not assess the outcome or context associated with the violent act (Berk et al., 1988; Browning & Dutton, 1986).

5. On a few occasions the researcher observed the officers completing the questionnaire when a senior officer would loudly remind his officers about the new legislation presuming arrest. In response, some of the officers would change their answers. In an effort to counter this, answers from the 31 officers (10%) who upgraded one or more of their responses (as indicated from the questionnaire form) were excluded from the analysis. This procedure therefore errs on the side of caution.

6. Sometimes the CAD records contained missing data on some of these variables, thereby accounting for differences in number of cases.

7. While the importance of the offender's presence at the scene in police officers' decision to arrest may at first strike as tautological, it is probably because this seems so simple that it has regularly escaped the scrutiny of researchers. For instance, one study investigating this variable (Feder, 1996) found that offender's presence was *more* important in explaining an arrest decision than the extent of victim's injuries. And, while the police knew the identity of the offender in most all of these cases, level of injury did not significantly increase the chance that the police would even attempt to contact the absent offender. Therefore, a domestic violence offender could easily escape all legal sanctions merely by not being present when police arrived.

8. With some injury being those cuts or bruises which do not result in a hospitalization and great injury defined as requiring a hospitalization.

BIBLIOGRAPHY

Balos, Beverly & Trotzky, Katie. (1988). Enforcement of the domestic abuse act in Minnesota: A preliminary study. *Law & Inequality, 6*, pp. 83-125.

Belknap, Joanne & McCall, K. Douglas. (1994). Woman battering and police referrals. *Journal of Criminal Justice, 22*(3), pp. 223-236.

Belknap, Joanne. (1995). Law enforcement officers' attitudes about the appropriate response to woman battering. *International Review of Victimology, 4*, pp. 47-62.

Bell, Daniel. (1985). Domestic violence: Victimization, police intervention, and disposition. *Journal of Criminal Justice, 13*, pp. 525-534.

Berk, Sarah F. & Loseke, Donileen. (1980-81). "Handling" family violence: Situational determinants of police arrest in domestic disturbances. *Law and Society Review, 15*(2), pp. 317-346.

Berk, Richard, Fenstermaker, Sarah, & Newton, Phyllis. (1988). An empirical analysis of police responses to incidents of wife battering. In G. Hotaling, D. Finkelhor, J. Kirkpatrick, & M. Straus (Eds.), *Coping with family violence: Research and policy perspectives* (pp. 158-168). Newbury Park, CA: Sage Publications.

Black, Donald. (1978). Production of crime rates. In L. Savitz & N. Johnston (Eds.), *Crime in society* (pp. 45-60). New York: John Wiley & Sons.

Blount, William, Yegidis, Bonnie, & Maheux, Randolp. (1992). Police attitudes toward preferred arrest: Influences of rank and productivity. *American Journal of Police, 9*(3), pp. 35-52.

Bowker, Lee. (1982). Police services to battered women: Bad or not so bad? *Criminal Justice and Behavior, 9*(4), pp. 476-494.

Breci, Michael. (1989). The effect of training on police attitudes toward family violence: Where does mandatory arrest fit in? *Journal of Crime and Justice, 12*(1), pp. 35-49.

Breci, Michael & Simons, Ronald. (1987). An examination of organizational and individual factors that influence police response to domestic disturbances. *Journal of Police Science and Administration, 15*(2), pp. 93-104.

Brown, Stephen. (1984). Police responses to wife beating: Neglect of a crime of violence. *Journal of Criminal Justice, 12*(3), 277-288.

Browning, James & Dutton, Donald. (1986). Conflict Tactics Scale: Using couple data to Quantify the differential reporting effect. *Journal of Marriage and the Family, 48*(2), pp. 375-379.

Buzawa, Eva. (1982). Police officer response to domestic violence legislation in Michigan. *Journal of Police Science and Administration, 10*(4), pp. 415-424.

Buzawa, Eve & Buzawa, Carl. (1985). Legislative trends in the criminal justice response to domestic violence. In A Lincoln & M. Straus (Eds.), *Crime in the family* (pp. 134-147). Springfield, IL: Charles C. Thomas.

Buzawa, Eve. (1988) Explaining variations in police response to domestic violence: A case study in Detroit and New England. In G. Hotaling, D. Finklhor, J. Kirkpatrick & M. Straus (Eds.), *Coping with family violence: Research and policy perspectives* (pp. 169-182). Newbury Park, Calif: Sage Publications.

Buzawa, Eve & Austin, Thomas. (1993). Determining police response to domestic violence victims. *American Behavioral Scientist, 36*(5), pp. 610-623.

Davidson, Terry. (1977). Wifebeating: A recurring phenomenon throughout history. In M. Roy (Ed.), *Battered women: A psychosociolgical study of domestic violence* (pp. 2-23). New York: Van Nostrand Reinhold.

Davis, Phillip. (1981). Structured rationales for non-arrest: Police stereotypes of the domestic disturbance. *Criminal Justice Review, 6*(2), pp. 8-15.

Davis, Phillip. (1983). Restoring the semblance of order: Police strategies in the domestic disturbance. *Symbolic Interaction, 6*(2), pp. 261-278.

Dolon, Ronald, Hendricks, James & Meagher, Steven. (1986). Police practices and attitudes toward domestic violence. *Journal of Police Science and Administration, 14*(3), pp. 187-192.

Dunford, Franklyn, Huizinga, David & Elliot, Delbert. (1990). The role of arrest in domestic assault: The Omaha Police Experiment. *Criminology, 28*(2), pp. 183-206.

Dutton, Donald. (1987). The criminal justice response to wife assault. *Law and Human Behavior, 11*(3), 189-206.

Dutton, Donald. (1988). Research advances in the study of wife assault: Etiology and prevention. *Law and Mental Health, 4,* 161-220.

Eigenberg, Helen, Scarborough, Kathryn & Kappeler, Victor. (1996). Contributory factors affecting arrest in domestic and non-domestic assaults. *American Journal of Police, 15*(4), pp. 27-54.

Erez, Edna. (1986). Intimacy, violence, and the police. *Human Relations, 39*(3), pp. 265-281.

Feder, Lynette. (1996). The importance of offender's presence in the arrest decision when police respond to domestic violence calls. *Journal of Criminal Justice, 12*(2), 279-305.

Feder, Lynette. (1997). Domestic violence and police response in a pro-arrest jurisdiction. *Women & Criminal Justice, 8*(4), 79-98.

Feder, Lynette. (1998). Police handling of domestic violence calls: Is there a case for discrimination? *Crime & Delinquency, 44*(2), pp. 139-153.

Ferraro, Kathleen. (1989). Policing woman battering. *Social Problems, 36*(1), pp. 61-74.

Friedman, Lucy & Shulman, Minna. (1990). Domestic violence: The criminal justice response. In A. Lurigio, W. Skogan, & R. Davis (Eds.), *Victims of crime: Problems, policies, and Programs* (pp. 87-103). Newbury Park, Calif: Sage Publications.

Gondolf, Edward, & McFerron, J. Richard. (1989). Handling battering men: Police action in wife abuse cases. *Criminal Justice & Behavior, 16*(4), 429-439.

Greenblat, Cathy. (1985). "Don't hit your wife. . . unless. . .": Preliminary findings on normative support for the use of physical force by husbands. *Victimology: An International Journal, 10*(1-4), pp. 221-241.

Hirschel, J. David, Hutchison, Ira, & Dean, Charles. (1992). The failure of arrest to deter spouse abuse. *Journal of Research in Crime and Delinquency, 29*(1), pp. 7-33.

Homant, Robert & Kennedy, Daniel. (1985). Police perceptions of spouse abuse: A comparison of male and female officers. *Journal of Criminal Justice, 13,* pp. 29-47.

Jaffe, Peter, Wolfe, David, Telford, Anne, & Austin, Gary. (1986). The impact of police charges in incidents of wife abuse. *Journal of Family Violence, 1*(1), 37-49.

Kennedy, Daniel & Homant, Robert. (1983). Attitudes of abused women toward male and female police officers. *Criminal Justice and Behavior, 10*(4), pp. 391-405.

Lawrenz, Frances, Lembo, James, & Schade, Thomas. (1988). Time series analysis of the effect of a domestic violence directive on the number of arrests per day. *Journal of Criminal Justice, 16,* pp. 493-498.

Lerman, Lisa. (1982). Court decisions on wife abuse laws: Recent developments. *Response to Family Violence and Sexual Assault, 5*(3-4), pp. 3-4 & 21-22.

Mederer, Helen & Gelles, Richard. (1989). Compassion or control: Intervention in cases of wife abuse. *Journal of Interpersonal Violence, 4*(1), pp. 25-43.

Oppenlander, Nan. (1982). Coping or copping out. *Criminology, 20*(3-4), pp. 449-465.

Saunders, Daniel & Size, Patricia. (1986). Attitudes about woman abuse among police officers, victims and victim advocates. *Journal of Interpersonal Violence, 1*(1), pp. 25-42.

Sherman, Lawrence, & Berk, Richard. (1984). The specific deterrent effects of arrest for domestic assault. *American Sociological Review, 49*, 261-272.

Sherman, Lawrence. (1988). *Domestic violence*. Washington, D.C.: U.S. Department of Justice, National Institute of Justice.

Sherman, Lawrence & Cohn, Ellen. (1989). The impact of research on legal policy: The Minneapolis Domestic Violence Experiment. *Law & Society Review, 23*(1), pp. 117-144.

Smith, Douglas & Visher, Christy. (1981). Street-level justice: Situational determinants of police arrest decisions. *Social Problems, 29*(2), pp. 167-177.

Smith, Douglas & Klein, Jody. (1984). Police control of interpersonal disputes. *Social Problems, 31*(4), pp. 468-481.

Smith, Douglas. (1987). Police response to interpersonal violence: Defining the parameters of legal control. *Social Forces, 65*(3), pp. 767-782.

Steinman, Michael. (1990). Lowering recidivism among men who batter women. *Journal of Police Science and Administration, 17*(2), pp. 124-132.

Stith, Sandra. (1990). The relationship between the male police officer's response to victims of domestic violence and his personal and family experiences. In E. Viano (Ed.), *The victimology handbook* (pp. 77-93). New York: Garland Publishing.

Stith, Sandra. (1990). Police response to domestic violence: The influence of individual and familial factors. *Violence and Victims, 5*(1), pp. 37-49.

Straus, Murray. (1977-78). Wife beating: How common and why? *Victimology: An International Journal, 2*, 443-458.

Taub, Nadine. (1983). Adult domestic violence: The law's response. *Victimology: An International Journal, 8*(1-2), pp. 152-171.

Waaland, Pam, & Keeley, Stuart. (1985). Police decision making in wife abuse: The impact of legal and extralegal factors. *Law and Human Behavior, 9*(4), 355-366.

Walter, James. (1981). Police in the middle: A study of small city police intervention in domestic disputes. *Journal of Police Science and Administration, 9*, pp. 243-260.

Worden, Robert & Pollitz, Alissa. (1984). Police arrests in domestic disturbances: A further look. *Law and Society Review, 18*(1), pp. 105-119.

Does Batterer Treatment Reduce Violence?
A Synthesis of the Literature

Robert C. Davis
Bruce G. Taylor

SUMMARY. This paper reviews three questions based upon the research literature on group treatment programs for batterers: (1) Does treatment reduce violence relative to the absence of treatment, (2) Do some forms of treatment work better than others, and (3) Does treatment work better for some batterers than for others? While there exist several dozen evaluations of batterer treatment programs, few have employed methodologies which are appropriate to addressing the issue of whether treatment is effective. However, among the handful of quasi- and true experiments there is fairly consistent evidence that treatment works and that the effect of treatment is substantial. Regarding the second question, we have little evidence to date that one form of treatment is superior to another or that longer programs turn out less violent graduates than shorter ones. Regarding the last question, there are bases for hypothesizing that some batterers may fare better in treatment (or fare better in certain types of treatment) than others. However, empirical verification has been highly limited to date. The paper concludes with lessons drawn from the literature on designing future research. *[Article copies available for a fee from The Haworth Document Delivery Service: 1-800-342-9678. E-mail address: getinfo@haworthpressinc.com]*

Robert C. Davis, MS, and Bruce G. Taylor, PhD, Senior Research Associates, Victim Services Research, 346 Broadway, Suite 206, New York, NY 10013.

The authors thank Joel Garner for making valuable comments on an earlier draft of this paper.

The views expressed are the authors' own and are not meant to represent the official position of Victim Services, the U.S. Department of Justice, or the National Institute of Justice.

[Haworth co-indexing entry note]: "Does Batterer Treatment Reduce Violence? A Synthesis of the Literature." Davis, Robert C. and Bruce G. Taylor. Co-published simultaneously in *Women & Criminal Justice* (The Haworth Press, Inc.) Vol. 10, No. 2, 1999, pp. 69-93; and: *Women and Domestic Violence: An Interdisciplinary Approach* (ed: Lynette Feder) The Haworth Press, Inc., 1999, pp. 69-93. Single or multiple copies of this article are available for a fee from The Haworth Document Delivery Service [1-800-342-9678, 9:00 a.m. - 5:00 p.m. (EST). E-mail address: getinfo@haworthpressinc.com].

Over the past two decades, the law enforcement response to domestic violence has become increasingly tough. Pro-arrest police policies have been promoted by advocates and widely adopted by police departments across the country (Buzawa and Buzawa, 1996). Increasingly, prosecutors as well have removed discretion traditionally given victims of domestic violence and insisted that cases be pursued to conviction regardless of victim desires or willingness to cooperate (Rebovich, 1996; Hanna, 1996). These changes have meant that criminal courts have had to sanction an expanding pool of batterers, and they have increasingly come to rely upon group treatment programs as the sanction of choice.

There are compelling reasons why group treatment programs for batterers have become a popular mode of court sanction. Even in serious battering cases, many victims choose to stay with abusive partners (Taylor, 1995). Such victims are interested in sanctions which offer them safety from violence, not retribution or punishment that will jeopardize their partner's ability to earn a living. Alternative sanctions commonly used in other crimes have little face validity in abuse cases: There is little reason to believe that fines, community service or probation without special conditions will stop batterers from abusing their spouses.

In this paper, we review research studies on the effectiveness of batterer treatment programs in reducing violence. We begin by reviewing the variety of treatment programs available. In the second section, we review evidence on whether batterer treatment reduces violence. The third section discusses research which compares outcomes of different types of treatment programs. In the fourth section, we synthesize what we have learned from the literature. The final section makes recommendations for future research.

I. THE NATURE OF BATTERER TREATMENT

The first group programs for batterers were begun during the late 1970s. Feminists, victim advocates, and others realized that providing services to victims of abuse and then returning them to the same home environment did little to solve abuse problems (Healey, Smith, and O'Sullivan, 1997). Group treatment was believed to be more appropriate than individual counseling or marital therapy because it expanded the social networks of batterers to include peers who are supportive of being nonabusive (Crowell and Burgess, 1996). Groups also proved to be less expensive than one-on-one counseling sessions. The earliest batterer groups were educational groups which sought to promote an anti-sexist message (Gondolf, 1995). With the passage of time, they gradually incorporated cognitive/behavioral therapeutic techniques and skill-building exercises.

As states introduced pro-arrest statutes during the 1980s the number of batterers arrested and convicted increased, and group treatment became the treatment of choice for the courts (Healey et al., 1997). Court-mandated batterer treatment significantly increased and diversified the number of batterer programs nationally (Feazell, Mayers, & Deschner, 1984). A recent estimate places the proportion of court mandates in treatment programs at 80% (Healey et al., 1997).

Batterer treatment may be required by criminal courts as part of a pre-trial diversion program, may be ordered by judges as part of a sentence, or may be imposed by probation agencies empowered to set special conditions of probation (Hamberger & Hastings, 1993). In at least one major urban jurisdiction, the district attorney sometimes agrees not to file charges at all if a brief treatment program is completed (Davis and Smith, 1997). In some states (see Ganley, 1987), civil courts as well as criminal may mandate a batterer to treatment (e.g., as a condition related to child visitation). Many batterer programs are run by probation departments, while others are run by mental health clinics, family service organizations, and victim service organizations.

Modern batterer groups tend to mix different theoretical approaches to treatment (Healey et al., 1997), although most batterer programs are based upon the feminist model developed by the Domestic Abuse Intervention Project in Duluth, Minnesota. The Duluth model assumes that physical violence is part of a spectrum of male efforts to control women. But batterer programs also commonly deal with the need for anger control, stress management, and better communication skills.

Not only treatment approach, but treatment length varies from program to program. The duration or number of sessions may vary from as little as one day to 32 weeks (Feazel et al., 1984). Some in the field even have advocated long-term treatment from 1 to 5 years (Ewing, Lindsey, & Pomerantz, 1984). However, there also is substantial pressure to keep batterer treatment short in duration resulting from pressure from insurance companies' imposition of time limits for batterers seeking reimbursement (Edelson and Syers, 1990).

Current trends in treatment programs seem to be going in conflicting directions. Increasingly, states are developing guidelines to codify standards for treatment content and length among batterer treatment programs (Gondolf, 1995). But, on the other hand, there is increasing sentiment that a "one-size fits all" approach to batterer treatment fails to recognize the diversity of batterers that enter treatment (Healey et al., 1997). There is a trend for treatment programs to tailor interventions to different batterer types defined by personality, violence history, or substance abuse. Other programs have been specially designed to accommodate sociocultural differences among batterers such as poverty, ethnicity, or sexual orientation.

II. DOES BATTERER TREATMENT WORK?

Over the last two decades there have been many empirical studies on batterer treatment programs. There are at least six published reviews of over 35 published single-site evaluations (Eisikovits & Edleson, 1989; Gondolf, 1991, 1995; Rosenfield, 1992; Saunders, 1996a; Tolman & Bennett, 1990) and eight book chapters reviewing this same research (e.g., Hamberger & Hastings, 1993; Crowell & Burgess, 1996; Dobash, Dobash, Cavanagh & Lewis, 1995; Dutton, 1988, 1995; Rosenbaum & O'Leary, 1986; Saunders & Azar, 1989; Tolman & Edleson, 1995). Since these literature reviews a number of new studies have been conducted and published.

However, the volume of the literature is deceptive. In fact, there have been only a handful of investigations that can make any legitimate claims about differences between treated batterers and untreated batterers. The batterer treatment literature has gone through three generations of studies. Most recent have been investigations which have randomly assigned batterers to treatment conditions. These are the strongest designs. Quasi-experiments of varying quality appeared somewhat earlier in the literature. The oldest, and by far the largest, portion of the empirical literature consists of studies which examine only batterers assigned to treatment programs. Included in this set of studies (which are discussed later in the paper) are: (a) studies which assess violence or other individual outcomes only after batterer treatment, (b) studies which measure violence before and after treatment, and (c) studies which compare violence of batterers who complete treatment with batterers assigned to treatment, but do not attend. Although the methodologies of early studies do not tend to be strong, they are important because they laid the foundation upon which stronger designs could be developed.

Methodological Issues in the Literature

In order to intelligently evaluate treatment outcome studies, it is important to have in mind some of the methodological shortcomings common in this literature. This section outlines some of the major problems which are common to many studies. These methodological issues have already been reviewed extensively elsewhere (e.g., Hamberger & Hastings, 1993; Rosenfeld, 1992 ; Saunders, 1996). However, a brief overview is necessary since we will draw upon this understanding to evaluate particular investigations and groups of studies.

First, there has been a lack of consensus on how to measure program effects. Studies have measured program effects on violence using official data on arrests and complaints, victim surveys, and batterer surveys. Rosenfeld's (1992) review makes the point in detail that official reports of violence and batterer surveys seriously underestimate actual violence committed in relationships. Moreover, some studies (e.g., Mauiro, Cahn, Vitaliano, and Zegree 1987) have not included any indicators of violence in their outcome measures. (Such studies are not included in our review.) Follow-up intervals have varied greatly, from several months to several years (Rosenfelds' 1992).

Studies differ widely in their statistical sophistication. While most have reported inferential statistics examining differences between means, a few have merely presented percentage differences (see Tables 1-3). Some studies which did use inferential statistics were conducted without sufficient statistical power to detect differences between treated and untreated participants (e.g., Chen et al., 1989). Some of the best quasi-experiments have incorporated multivariate analyses which attempt to control for the effects of extraneous variables when isolating effects (Harrell, 1991).

Studies have varied in terms of the populations they are investigating. Obviously, the samples in these studies are not going to be representative of all batterers in the United States, or even all batterers mandated to batterer treatment in the United States. Most researchers would probably be satisfied with demonstrating that batterer programs are effective for some well-defined group of batterers in a court system, in one city. Clearly, obvious sample selection biases should be avoided.

One such sample selection bias is that most of the batterer programs that have been evaluated exclude difficult batterers (e.g., recidivist batterers or those who have substance abuse problems) from their programs (see Rosenfeld, 1992 for a review). Elimination of potentially difficult subjects may overestimate the successfulness of treatment programs, were these programs forced to accept these more difficult cases (Rosenfeld, 1992). Therefore, the results of many of these studies may apply only to a limited spectrum of batterers.

The problem of generalizeability of results also crops up in another way. Many treatment studies which have relied on batterer or victim surveys to assess violence have had poor interview response rates, some as low as 30% (see Edelson and Syers, 1990 for a review). Low response rates are a problem because the cases in which follow-up data are available may be different than those cases in which data are not available. For example, Edleson and Syers (1990) reported higher levels of education and income for batterers who completed follow-up surveys compared to batterers who did not do a follow-up survey. It is unclear, therefore, whether their analysis of treatment effects applies to the low SES batterers who failed to complete the survey as well as the higher SES batterers who did complete it.

Finally, batterer treatment programs have serious problems with attrition: Many evaluations report that fewer than half of batterers assigned to treatment, in fact, completed the program (see Eisikovits & Edleson, 1989 for a more extensive review of attrition rates). Low treatment completion rates present researchers conducting experiments or quasi-experiments with a dilemma. If they compare only batterers who complete treatment with batterers not assigned to treatment, they are subject to criticisms of "creaming." That is, they are comparing the best of the treatment group (the most highly motivated batterers) with untreated batterers, thereby stacking the deck in favor of finding program effects. On the other hand, if all batterers assigned to treatment are included in the comparison, yet most failed to complete treatment, they are subject to the criticism that their study is biased against finding program effects. In other words, program effects would have to be very large, indeed, to show up after being diluted by inclusion of drop-outs who were not exposed to the treatment (or exposed to a lesser treatment "dosage").

Studies Without a Comparison Group

Non-Experimental One Group Post-Test only Designs

At least 15 published studies have used designs which generate a single measure of treatment effectiveness: violence following completion of treatment (see Table 1). Ten measured recidivism based only upon batterer self-reports. Only four of the fifteen studies had substantial sample sizes (which we have arbitrarily defined as greater than 100) or lengthy follow-up periods (which we have defined as one year or greater).

Recidivism rates in this group of studies vary widely, from 7% to 47% (mean 26%). Interpretation of results is difficult at best without a comparison group or pre-test information with which to compare outcome measures.

Non-Experimental One Group Pre-Test and Post-Test Designs

At least seven published studies compared violence among treated batterers after program participation to violence levels prior to participation (see Table 2). Three of the seven studies included both victim and batterer self-reports, but just two had follow-up periods of at least a year and none of the studies examined police records. Two of the seven studies had sample sizes greater than 100. Of the six studies that reported treatment attrition rates, four of the studies had attrition rates of 25% or less.

All seven studies reported lower recidivism rates following treatment (but results of one study were not statistically significant; two studies did not report probability statistics). However, with this type of design, reductions in recidivism cannot be attributed necessarily to the effects of treatment. This is true because studies have repeatedly shown that domestic violence declines after the police are called, *even if nothing else is done*. In fact, research suggests that only about a third of batterers commit repeat domestic violence within the next six months after the police intervene (see, for example, Davis

TABLE 1. Batterer Treatment Evaluations Using a Post-Test only Design

Authors of Study	Sample Size	Data Source	Follow-Up Time	Recidivism	Attrition
Purdy & Nickle (1981)	170	Batterer	6 months	41%	Unknown
Deschner (1984)	12	Batterer	8 months	15%	50%
Feazel, Mayers, and Deschner (1984)	90	Batterer	1 Year	25%	Unknown
Edleson, Miller, Stone, and Chapman (1985)	9	Batterer	7 to 21 weeks	22%	0%
Neidig, Friedman, and Collins (1985)	Unknown	Batterer	4 months	13%	Unknown
Harris (1986)	40	Batterer	2 months to 3 years	27%	Unknown
DeMaris and Jackson (1987)	53	Batterer	20 months	35%	83%
Leong, Coates, and Hoskins (1987)	67	Victim, Police	3 months	19% (Victim) 15% (Police)	76%
Shupe, Stacey & Hazlewood (1987)	148	Victim, Batterer	3 months to a few years	30% (Victim) 18% (Batterer)	31%
Tolman, Beeman, and Mendoza (1987)	48	Victim	6 months	47%	68%
Edleson and Grusznski (1988) (Study 2)	86	Victim	9 months	33%	0%
Beninati (1989)	16	Batterer	Unknown	19%	25%
Hamberger and Hastings (1990)	106	Batterer	1 year	30%	16%
Johnson and Kanzler (1990)	687	Batterer	5 months	7%	30%
Tolman and Bhosley (1991)	99	Victim	1 year	42%	50%

and Taylor, 1997b; Sherman, 1992; Fagan, Friedman, Wexler, and Lewis 1984). The post-treatment violence rates displayed in Table 2 also average about one-third–in other words not different than one might expect even if the batterers had not undergone treatment.

Comparing Treatment Drop-Outs versus Completers

Six studies compared outcomes between batterers who completed treatment and batterers assigned to a treatment program, but who failed to complete treatment (see Table 3). Four of the six studies had sample sizes under 100. Only two of the six studies had follow-up periods of at least one year, and just one included more than a single measure of recidivism.

TABLE 2. One Group Pre and Post-Test Design

Authors of Study	Sample Size	Data Source	Follow-Up Time	Recidivism	Attrition
Dutton (1986) Part 1	50	Batterer & Victim	6 months to 3 years	Pre-Test 13.4 All DV acts (Batterer reports)/ Post-Test 4.6 All DV acts (Batterer reports) Pre-Test 21.3 All DV acts (Victim reports)/ Post-Test 6.1 All DV acts (Victim reports) (For all differences, P < .05)	10%
Rosenbaum (1986)	11	Batterer	4 & 6 months	100% (Pre-treatment) 9% (4 months) 27% (6 months) (P < .05)	18%
Waldo (1986)	23	Batterer	6 months	Pre-test 5.1 DV acts/ Post-test 0.29 DV acts (P < .05)	Unknown
Shepard (1987)	92	Batterer	14 months	Pre-Test 39%/Post-Test 30% (Statistical significance not reported)	25%
Hamberger and Hastings (1988) Part 1	35	Batterer, Victim (Combined measure)	1 year	Pre-Test 20.9 DV acts/ Post-Test 5.3 DV acts (P < .001)	0%
Meredith & Burns (1990)	125	Batterer, Victim	3 months	Physical, verbal & emotional abuse all reduced at post-test (% not reported)	53%

The most serious flaw in these six studies is that the treated and untreated (dropout) groups are almost certainly not comparable in complex ways prior to treatment. As pointed out by Palmer, Brown, and Barrera (1992), attendance is a confounding factor because better attendance is likely an indication of higher motivation to change, even before treatment. Therefore, differential recidivism between program completers and drop-outs could be due to motivational differences in the two groups that existed prior to treatment. Surprisingly, however, only one of the six studies reported significantly lower recidivism rates for the completers (four of the other five studies were in the predicted direction but either had results that were not statistically significant or did not include inferential statistics).

The best use of this group of studies is to describe the characteristics of people that drop out of treatment–information potentially useful to program developers to improve batterer groups. Results have indicated that those who do not complete treatment are more likely to be victims of child abuse (Grusznki & Carrillo, 1988), unemployed (Hamberger & Hastings, 1988), uneducated (Grusznki & Carrillo, 1988), young (Hamberger & Hastings,

TABLE 3. Quasi-Experiment (Dropouts versus Completers)

Authors of Study	Sample Size	Data Source	Follow-Up Time	Recidivism
Halpern (1984)	84	Victim	3 months	18% dropouts/15% completers (N.S.)
Hawkins & Beauvais (1985)	106	Police	6 months	18% dropouts/18% completers (N.S.)
Douglas & Perrin (1987)	40	Police	6 months	29% dropouts/15% completers (No Statistics Reported)
Edleson and Grusznski (1988, Study 1)	86	Victim	About 5 to 9 months	46% dropouts/32% completers (P < .03)
Edleson and Grusznski (1988, Study 3)	159	Victim	1 year	48% dropouts/41% completers (N.S.)
Hamberger and Hastings (1988) Part 2	71	Batterer, Victim, Police (Combined measure)	1 year	47% dropouts/28% completers (P < .06)

1993), psychologically disturbed (Hamberger & Hastings, 1989; Grusznki & Carrillo, 1988), and substance abusers (Hamberger & Hastings, 1990).

Quasi-Experimental Non-Equivalent Matched Groups

We found four studies in which batterers mandated to treatment by the courts were compared to batterers who received other interventions. This group of studies is the first we have examined which addressed in a rigorous fashion the issue of whether treatment works. There is a notable difference in design details between these four quasi-experiments and the other studies reviewed thus far. All four of the studies had sample sizes greater than 100 (see Table 4). None of the studies relied solely on batterer self-reports. All four had follow-up periods of at least one year.

The first quasi-experiment was reported by Dutton (1986). His sample consisted of 100 convicted batterers on probation. He compared 50 batterers who were treated within a cognitive-behavioral group model to 50 batterers who were not designated to receive treatment. The treatment group had a 4% recidivism rate compared to 40% for the control group based upon police reports. However, although Dutton reports that groups did not differ on several demographic measures, pre-treatment comparability of the groups is highly suspect: The control group was composed of batterers whom probation officers did not select for treatment, some of whom were explicitly rejected by therapists as unsuitable for treatment. The treatment group con-

TABLE 4. Quasi-Experiment (Matched Control Group)

Authors of Study	Sample Size	Data Source	Follow-Up Time	Recidivism	Attrition
Dutton (1986) Part 2	100	Police	6 months to 3 years	40% No treatment/ 4% Treatment (P < .001)	0%
Chen, Bersani, Myers, and Denton (1989)	221	Police	Average of 14 months	10% (0.53 DV acts) No treatment/ 5% (0.35 DV acts) Treatment (P < .05) Perps Attended > 75% TX less recidivism than controls (P < .05)	Unknown
Harrell (1991)	348	Batterer/ Victim (Combined measure), Police	6 months for batterer & victims, 15 and 29 months for police	15% severe violence No Treatment/20% Treatment (P = N.S.), 12% physical aggression No TX/ 43% Treatment (P < .01) 7% New DV charges No Treatment/ 19% Treatment (P < .05)	24%
Dobash et al. (1996)	313	Victim & Court Reports	3 to 12 months	7% treated, 10% untreated (court reports 12 months) 30% treated, 62% untreated (victim 3 months) 33% treated, 75% untreated (victim 12 months) No probability statistics provided	Unknown

sisted of only batterers who *completed* the treatment program. Dutton does not report what proportion of all batterers assigned to treatment dropped out but, based on other work, we have to assume that it was a large proportion.

Chen et al. (1989) conducted a quasi-experiment involving 120 batterers assigned to treatment by the courts and 101 comparison batterers drawn from court calendars who were not mandated to go to treatment. (No details are given on how the controls were selected or what the outcomes were of their court cases, although the authors state that the samples proved to be well-matched demographically.) Sixty-three percent of the men assigned to treatment completed at least 75% of the required sessions. Chen et al. also used a sophisticated data analytic technique (selection bias modeling) to deal with the potential non-equivalence of groups prior to treatment inherent in non-randomized experiments. They found that, after an average of 14 months, 5% of batterers assigned to treatment had been rearrested compared to 10% of controls. The main effect of the treatment variable was not statistically significant, although the authors noted that batterers who completed at least 75% of the requisite sessions had significantly lower rates of recidivism than controls.

Harrell (1991) studied 227 batterers, 115 of whom were ordered to treatment by judges. (She does not specify what court outcomes of the untreated group were.) Her attempt to obtain equivalency between those treated batterers controls hinged on a quirk in the court she studied. She noted that treatment program referrals came almost exclusively from a small group of judges; other judges seldom mandated treatment for batterers. Therefore, she drew her comparison group from the caseloads of judges who seldom referred to the treatment program. However, her plan did not work as she had intended. Harrell found three important and statistically significant differences between treated batterers and controls. (The former were more likely to be married to their partners and employed, and less likely to have a criminal record.) While she controlled for these variables in her analysis of recidivism effects, it is quite possible that there were additional, unmeasured differences between the groups.

Harrell's analysis included only batterers in the treatment group who actually completed treatment. Comparisons of recidivism were based on a combined measure of the victim and perpetrator reports of violence six months after case disposition. In addition, police records were reviewed 15-29 months after case disposition. Surprisingly, a significantly larger percentage of those in the treatment group committed new violence than those in the control group for two of three measures that she reports. (The third measure is in the same direction, but not statistically significant.) For example, 7% of the control group and 19% of the treatment group were charged with new domestic crimes. While Harrell's study may be limited in its ability to distinguish between selection effects and treatment effects, it certainly adds controversy to the debate about the efficacy of treatment programs.

Recently, Dobash, Emerson-Dobash, Cavanagh and Lewis (1996) reported on a quasi-experiment evaluating a treatment program in Great Britain. Dobash et al. examined 256 domestic violence cases from sheriffs' courts in Scotland in which defendants were sentenced to batterer treatment or to another sentence (probation, court supervision, or prison). Few details are given about how the control group was selected, but the authors note that batterers in the treatment group were significantly older and more likely to be employed than batterers in the control group. (These differences are reminiscent of pre-treatment differences in Harrell's study.)

It is not specified whether Dobash et al. included in their analyses all batterers assigned to treatment, or only those who completed treatment. According to court reports at 12 months follow-up, 7% of the treatment group recidivated compared to 10% of the control group; no statistical tests were reported to indicate whether the difference was significant. Data from victim surveys indicated that half as many batterers assigned to treatment committed new violence at three or 12 months as controls. (These two comparisons are reported to be statistically significant, although no specific information is provided.) However, the success rate for interviews was low: Dobash et al. interviewed only 43% of the victims at the first follow-up interview, 34% at the second interview, and 25% at the third interview.

Randomized Experiments

As pointed out by Palmer et al. (1992), quasi-experiments on batterer treatment cannot be relied upon to produce unbiased estimates of the effects of treatment. This is true because we cannot know whether batterers assigned to treatment and controls are equivalent prior to application of the treatment. In some quasi-experiments (such as the Dutton, 1986 or Harrell, 1991 studies), we know for certain that selection bias favored finding treatment effects (because the control group was comprised of batterers more prone to recidivate than those in the treated group).

It can be argued that initial differences between groups can be controlled statistically, but this is only true if all relevant initial differences are known to researchers. For example, a researcher may discover pre-treatment differences in employment, marital status, and criminal history between those assigned to batterer treatment and controls, and these differences may be statistically controlled in analyses. However, groups may well have differed on less tangible and more fundamental factors such as emotional maturity as well. If such factors are not controlled (because they are not known) and they are correlated with outcome measures, then the results of the study are uninterpretable. The safest way to ensure that estimates of sample means are unbiased is through random assignment of batterers to treatments.

Palmer et al. conducted the first experiment with random assignment to a true no treatment control group (see Table 5). The number of subjects in the experiment was far smaller than one would expect to need to detect treatment effects. Fifty-nine probationers were assigned using a "block random" procedure to either a ten-session psychoeducational group (combining group discussion with information) or a no treatment control group. Participants were assigned to treatment if a new group was to commence within three weeks; otherwise they became part of the control group. In only two cases was a defendant assigned to the control condition reassigned by court officials to the treatment condition. Attrition was kept within a respectable range: 70% of the men assigned to treatment attended at least seven of the required 10 sessions.

It is significant that this is one of the only studies to compare all batterers *assigned* to treatment (not just those who completed treatment) with controls. Palmer and her colleagues examined police reports six months post-treatment and found recidivism rates (domestic physical abuse or serious threats) for the treatment group to be just one-third that of the control group (10% compared

TABLE 5. Randomized Experiments

Authors of Study	Sample Size	Data Source	Follow-Up Time	Recidivism	Attrition
Palmer et al. (1992)	59	Police (100%) (for Batterer (n = 32) and Victim (n = 13) there are too few cases to analyze)	12 months (police data)	31% No Treatment/ 10% Treatment	30%
Feder (1996) (No data available yet)	600	Victim, Batterer, Poiice Records, Probation Records	6 months, 1 year	Not available yet	Not available yet
Davis and Taylor (1997)	376	Victim, Batterer (Not available yet), Police Complaint and Arrest Records	6 months 1 year (Not available yet)	12.9% No treatment/ 4.6% Treatment (P < .001) 20% No treatment/ 11% Treatment (P < .05) 2.03 acts of DV for No Treatment/ 0.89 acts of DV for Treatment (P < .05)	33%
Dunford (1997) (No data) available yet)	861	Victim, Batterer and Police Records	6 months, 1 year, 18 months, 2 years	Not available yet	Not available yet

to 31%). Even with the small N, this difference was statistically significant. While Palmer et al. attempted to generate additional violence measures from surveys of interviews and batterers, low response rates combined with a small N precluded any analysis of recidivism based upon interview data.

Davis and Taylor (1997a) conducted a larger experiment on batterer treatment in Brooklyn, NY. Three hundred seventy-six men who had pled guilty to domestic violence misdemeanors were randomly assigned to batterer treatment or were denied the opportunity to enter the treatment program. Treatment was 40 hours of batterer education based upon the Duluth model, conducted either over a 26-week or over an 8-week period. Those who were denied entrance to the program were sentenced to community service, a sanction not considered relevant to preventing spouse abuse.

Davis and Taylor had a sample size determined by a power analysis to be large enough to detect reasonable differences in outcomes between the groups and multiple measures of violence (based on victim and batterer interviews and official police records of new complaints and arrests collected six and 12 months post-sentencing). Cases were randomly assigned individually at the last possible point in the process–after prosecution, defense, and judge all had agreed on sending the defendant to the treatment program. (Officials were aware that half of the defendants determined appropriate for the program would be rejected by lottery, and all had agreed to community service in that event.) Although cases were randomly assigned to treatments, only a minority of domestic violence cases ever entered the assignment process because someone (usually the defense) failed to agree to accept a treatment program. Nonetheless, this study represents one of the few times in criminal justice research that defendants have been sentenced randomly for research purposes.

Preliminary analysis of six-month outcome data showed that 5% of the men assigned to batterer treatment were arrested for a new domestic violence offense compared to 13% of the batterers assigned to the control group. The second analysis, based on crime reports showed that 11% of the batterers assigned to treatment had police complaints for a new domestic violence offense filed against them compared to 20% of the batterers assigned to the control group. The third analysis, based on the victim data, showed no difference in prevalence of new violence. Victim reports did show, however, that batterers assigned to treatment committed on average fewer acts of domestic violence than batterers assigned to the control group (0.89 compared to 2.03).

Two additional randomized experiments are in progress. Dunford (1997) is in the final stages of comparing treatment outcomes for 861 legally married Navy couples in which physical abuse had come to the attention of Navy authorities. These cases were randomly assigned to one of four treatments, including (a) 26-week batterer treatment (based on a cognitive/behavioral model), (b) 26 weeks of couples counseling, (c) rigorous monitoring (including monthly calls to victims and semi-annual police record checks), and (d) establishing a safety plan for victims. The safety planning was intended by the investigators as a no-treatment control against which to compare the effects of the other three treatments. (Safety planning was given to victims in each of the other three conditions as well.) This would seem to be a fairly good no-treatment condition, in so far as the men in this condition received no intervention. Victims and batterers are being interviewed every six months over a period of two years. Feder (1996) has assigned batterers placed on probation to either a 26-week educational batterer program based on the Duluth model or a control group not mandated to treatment. Multiple measures of recidivism will be assessed (victim, batterer, police records, probation records) for six months and one year.

III. DOES ONE TYPE OF TREATMENT WORK BETTER THAN ANOTHER?

In this section, we turn our attention from studies which have addressed the question "Does treatment work?" to studies which have asked whether one mode of treatment is superior to another. In general, the studies in this section have used far stronger designs than those which have addressed the effectiveness of treatment. This is because it is easier for researchers to "sell" to practitioners a study in which everyone will receive some form of treatment than a study in which some batterers will not receive treatment. If, in the worst case scenario, a research participant kills his spouse, authorities can still maintain that he had received one of several appropriate interventions.

Harris, Savage, Jones, and Brooke (1988) randomly assigned 58 violent couples who presented themselves for marital counseling to ten weeks of either group or couple counseling. The authors state that they found no significant differences between the two conditions in women's reports of new violence six months to one year after they were assigned to treatment conditions. However, this conclusion is based upon just 28 of the 58 women whom they were able to contact for the interview. The authors noted that retention was much better (84%) in the group condition than in the couple condition (33%).

Edleson and Syers (1990) randomly assigned 283 batterers to one of three groups: An educational program, a self-help program, or a combined educational/self-help program. Each program was either 12 sessions in 12 weeks or 32 sessions in 16 weeks. Violence was assessed six months after treatment through interviews with victims and/or batterers. Edleson and Syers reported no significant differences between treatment modalities or between treatment lengths for their violence measure, but did find a significant advantage for the education model on a measure of terroristic threats. The authors do report that men who participated in education groups were the least likely to use terroristic threats during follow-up. However, because they included only program completers and cases with at least one complete interview in their analysis, their results are based upon just 92 of the original 283 cases.

Saunders (1996b) reported on the results of an experiment in which 218 men were randomly assigned to either feminist-cognitive-behavioral or process-psychodynamic group treatments. Saunders reports on 18-month violence measures (victim and batterer reports and arrest records) only for the 136 men who successfully completed the programs. No significant main effects of treatment modality were found (although Saunders did find a significant interaction of batterer type with treatment type–see below).

Goldkamp (1996) randomly assigned 350 domestic violence offenders with diagnosed substance abuse problems either to a batterer treatment program followed by substance abuse counseling or to an integrated batterer treatment-substance abuse program. Attrition was very different for experimentals (integrated model) and controls (sequential model): just 13% of experimentals failed to attend any treatment sessions, compared to 44% of controls. (No explanation is offered for this discrepancy.) Goldkamp's follow-up period was short–just seven months. As a result, 42% of the controls and 32% of experimentals had not completed treatment by the measurement point. He found overall rearrest rates of 23% for experimentals and 29% for controls. For domestic violence rearrests involving the same victim, the corresponding figures were 6% and 14%. Goldkamp does not say whether these figures are statistically significant.

Brannen and Rubin (1996) conducted another randomized experiment in which 49 court-referred couples were referred to one of two conditions. In the *couples group intervention* condition, couples attended together an educational group based on a cognitive-behavioral model. In the *gender-specific group intervention* condition, batterers attended Duluth model educational groups while victims attended empowerment groups. Violence was assessed based upon victim reports, although it is unclear *when* the assessments were carried out. Analyses showed no main effect of type of treatment: However, among batterers with a history of alcohol abuse, the couples approach led to reduced violence compared to the individual treatment approach.

Recently, Gondolf (1997a) reported on the results of a large (N = 840) multi-site comparison of four treatment programs. The programs varied in length and type of treatment provided, and included (a) a three-month didactic program, (b) a three-month process program with service for victims in addition, (c) a five-month didactic program, and (d) a nine-month process program with complementary services (substance abuse treatment, mental health counseling, and services for women). The men and their partners were interviewed every three months for 15 months and police records were checked. Gondolf reports that the overall 30% reassault rate did not vary across programs, giving him no basis to conclude that treatment length or modality affect recidivism.

Finally, the study in progress by Dunford (1997) reviewed in section II also will generate data comparing treatment modalities. Once again, Dunford's three treatment groups included a treatment program for batterers, couples counseling, and rigorous monitoring. The three treatments can be compared to each other as well as to a "no-treatment" condition in which victims received assistance in safety planning.

IV. SYNTHESIS OF EMPIRICAL FINDINGS

What have we learned to date about whether batterer treatment works? If we disallow studies without a comparison group (and we would strongly urge this course), we are left with results from four quasi- and two true experiments. Five of the six (Harrell et al. is the lone exception) reported results in the expected direction and all reported statistical significance on at least one outcome measure.

But even more important are the effect sizes from these investigations.

Effect size has been argued to be a more important index of treatment effects than statistical significance (e.g., Cohen, 1992; Rosenthal, 1991). It provides a measure of detectability of an effect which is independent of the baseline rate to which it is being compared (Bem and Honorton, 1994). (The power to detect the difference between .55 and .25 is different from the power to detect the difference between .50 and .20.)

We computed effect sizes for five of the six quasi- and true experiments reviewed in this paper. (Harrell et al.'s anomalous work was omitted from this analysis.) The effect sizes were computed on proportions of repeat violence culled from police records because it was the most commonly available measure from this group of studies. Effect size was assessed using Cohen's *h* (Cohen, 1988). In the five batterer treatment studies that found evidence in favor of treatment, effect sizes ranged from 0.108 to 0.946 (see Table 6). To place these effect sizes in context, consider the effect size of one of the early large clinical trials on the effect of aspirin on heart attack rates. In that research, more than 22,000 subjects were randomly assigned to take aspirin or a placebo. The study was stopped after six years because it was already clear that the aspirin treatment was effective (p < .00001) and today it is common medical practice for doctors to prescribe aspirin to prevent second heart attacks. Yet the effect size, as measured by Cohen's *h*, was only 0.068. Against this standard, the effect sizes seen in batterer treatment studies are quite substantial.

A common technique in meta-analysis is to give studies quality ratings and then correlate the ratings with effect sizes. If the effect size decreases as quality of the research goes up, it is a good indication that the effect is not real

TABLE 6. Treatment Effect Sizes for Quasi and True Experiments: Comparing Treatment to No Treatment

	Recidivism		
Quasi-Experiments	Treated	Untreated	**Effect Size**
Dutton (1986)	4%	40%	0.946
Chen et al. (1989)	5%	10%	0.193
Dobash et al. (1996)	7%	10%	0.108
Average			0.416

	Recidivism		
True-Experiments	Treated	Untreated	**Effect Size**
Palmer et al. (1992)	10%	31%	0.537
Davis and Taylor (1997)	5%	13%	0.287
Average			0.412

(see, for example, Utts, 1991). This has often been the case in criminal justice. For example, early literature on pretrial diversion was generally positive; but when a true experiment was conducted, no effect of diversion upon subsequent criminal behavior was found (Baker and Sadd, 1979).

In contrast, the effects do not seem to disappear in the batterer treatment literature as the studies become more rigorous. Referring to Table 6, it is clear that treatment effects do not decline as we move from quasi-experiments to true experiments. The average effect sizes for the two true experiments (0.412) is virtually identical to the average for the quasi-experiments (0.416).

Taken together, these studies provide a case for rejecting the null hypothesis that treatment has no effect on violent behavior toward spouses. However, the number of experimental and quasi-experimental studies is small and more methodologically rigorous studies are warranted before coming to firm conclusions.

Results to date do not suggest any difference in program effectiveness according to treatment modality or length of treatment program. The only exception to that generalization is Goldkamp's (1996) finding of lower recidivism in a concurrent batterer and substance abuse treatment group relative to sequential participation in separate batterer treatment and substance abuse programs. Current practices of many batterer treatment programs, which will not accept substance abusers unless they first have completed a substance abuse program, run contrary to Goldkamp's findings.

V. RECOMMENDATIONS FOR FUTURE RESEARCH

The evaluations that have been done can provide useful information to future researchers. From these studies, we have estimates of treatment effect size which can be used to determine appropriate sample sizes for future investigations. Researchers will not need to guess whether they need 50 cases or 500 cases in order to attain the requisite statistical power needed to detect real effects.

We recommend that several standards be applied to future investigations into whether treatment has an effect on violence. First, as recognized by Fagan (1996) and others, randomized experiments should be the design of choice. We recognize that random assignment when applied to judicial mandates to treatment are likely to prove difficult or impossible (since it is tantamount to sentencing by lottery and requires the agreement of prosecution, defense, and judiciary). However, true experimental designs are not unrealistic when applied to probationers who are mandated to treatment at the discretion of probation administrators. Jurisdictions in which treatment mandates are at the discretion of the probation agency are prime potential settings for conducting randomized experiments.*

Second, measures and follow-up intervals need to be standardized so that results can be compared across studies. Too many studies have relied only upon batterer self-reports, known to vastly underestimate the true incidence of abuse (for an expanded discussion of this point, see Rosenfeld, 1992). The same kinds of measurement standards used in the National Institute of Justice's Spouse Abuse Replication Project (SARP) studies ought to be applied to batterer treatment: Investigations ought to include victim reports, crime complaints made to the police, and arrests. Batterers ought to be tracked at six-month intervals for at least one year, and preferably two. Short-term measures are needed to assess immediate program effects–effects that may be transient. Longer-term follow-up is needed to determine whether treatment leads to permanent changes. The use of both short-term and long-term measures is especially important in light of the suggestions from some of the SARP sites that law enforcement intervention may have deterrent effects in the short-run, but facilitating effects on battering in the long run (for a discussion of measurement issues in the SARP data, see Garner, Fagan, and Maxwell, 1995).

Third, investigations of the effects of batterer treatment need to be explicit in defining the standard against which treatment is being evaluated. Too many studies have compared men who go through batterer treatment to men who receive unspecified other sentences in the courts. To gauge the effects of treatment compared to the absence of treatment, it is imperative that batterers in the control group receive nothing relevant to reducing their propensity to batter. This may be possible when using a sample of probationers, some of whom are assigned to batterer treatment in addition to regular supervision and others of whom are assigned only to normal supervision regimes.

Fourth, researchers need to find ways to minimize attrition from treatment programs. Batterer program attrition typically runs greater than half of all participants assigned to treatment. This poses a serious dilemma for researchers, who must choose between analyzing groups as assigned (that is comparing all individuals assigned to treatment to all individuals in the control condition) and comparing only program completers to controls. If treatment attrition is high, the first alternative results in overly conservative estimates of program effects since the treatment group is made up of many individuals exposed to minimal or no treatment. On the other hand, comparing only

---

*However, it should be noted that such a strategy could still be a challenge to implement. That is, the researcher would have to find a number of probation officers who were willing to follow random assignment procedures, and then carefully monitor their compliance on the issue of study "overrides" (as discussed earlier in this paper).

treatment completers to controls biases the analysis in favor of finding significant treatment effects since those who complete treatment are the "cream" of the group of batterers assigned to treatment.

Sherman (1992) argues that, assuming treatment attrition can be minimized, the clear preference is to "analyze as randomized." The critical question, according to Sherman, is whether the proportion of cases treated differently than the random assignment is larger than the proportion of cases with negative outcomes. On the one hand, analyzing according to treatments as assigned becomes a problem when the treatment often fails to be delivered. A high rate of treatment "crossovers" reduces statistical power and increases the likelihood that an effective treatment will go undetected (Gartin, 1995; Weinstein and Levin, 1989).

The best way out of this dilemma is to minimize treatment crossovers, most commonly attributable to treatment program attrition. Suggestions are that treatment attrition can be minimized by telescoping treatment into a short time span and by imposing penalties for failure to attend classes. Also, studying treatment programs located within corrections institutions–where batterers have no choice about attending sessions–would provide a way around the attrition problem. (However, using a batterer sample from prison would raise the issue of the generalizability of the results to non-prisoner batterer samples. Prisons and jail settings may contain very different types of batterers than the type of batterers seen in the typical non-prison batterer program.) Such an institutional setting would provide a vehicle to examine the "dosage-response curve" indicating how treatment outcomes vary according to the number of sessions batterers are exposed to. This issue is important in light of the trend toward longer treatment programs, as yet unsubstantiated by empirical findings indicating that lengthy programs work better than shorter ones.

Fifth, researchers ought to make explicit issues which may restrict the extent to which their findings can be generalized. Particular attention needs to be given to the sample of batterers who participate in a research study. Are they court-mandated? Do they have extensive prior criminal histories or not? Do defendants have a chance to volunteer for treatment or are they sent to treatment regardless of their willingness to participate? Also potentially important is the criminal justice context within which treatment studies are set. Treatment program effectiveness may vary according to local court practices, linkages between agencies, sanctions for non-compliance, and so forth.

Finally, researchers need to find ways to maximize interview response rates when interviewing victims about continuing abusive behavior from their spouses. It is common to have interview success rates around 50% when contacting victims six months or later (e.g., Feld & Straus, 1990). There are good reasons why rates are so low: researchers are interviewing victims who did not initially agree to participate, they must rely on inaccurate contact information from the files of criminal justice agencies, and domestic violence victims and offenders are notoriously transient. Nonetheless, with interview success rates of 50%, it is difficult to make the case that interview data are representative of the sample as a whole. However, with sophisticated methods of follow-up and judicious use of financial incentives, it should be possible to attain relatively respectable response rates (see Sullivan, Rumptz, Campbell, Eby, and Davidson, 1996 for a discussion of minimizing survey attrition with battered women samples).

There are parallels between the batterer treatment literature today and the literature on the rehabilitation of criminal offenders about 15 years ago. In both literatures, the problem is not too few studies, but a paucity of sophisticated research. Calls that were made years ago by the National Academy of Sciences (Martin, Sechrest, and Redner, 1981) for agreement on outcome measures and randomized experiments in rehabilitation are just as relevant today for batterer treatment. The evolution in sophistication of batterer treatment studies is encouraging. By using randomized experiments and other designs that have a high degree of internal validity, we soon should be able to say whether batterer treatment works and to specify which program models are most effective.

AUTHOR NOTE

Robert C. Davis is a consultant to the American Bar Association. He is the author of numerous journal articles, book chapters, and books. His recent publications have been on domestic violence, sexual assault, elder abuse, crime prevention, drug enforcement, and specialized courts. He is currently conducting two large field tests of treatment interventions for domestic violence, and a study on community policing in immigrant communities.

Bruce G. Taylor is working on research projects examining the effectiveness of batterer treatment, police and social service responses to domestic violence, psychological effects of victimization, and community policing in immigrant communities. He is finishing up several papers for publication on the results of his research at Victim Services, including a book for Sage Publications on the psychological effects of victimization. He also served as a consultant to the Administrative Office of the Courts of New Jersey and NDRI. He received his doctorate from Rutgers University, School of Criminal Justice in 1996.

REFERENCES

Adams, D. (1988). Counseling men who batter: A profeminist analysis of five treatment models. In M. Bograd & K. Yllo (Eds.), *Feminist perspectives on wife abuse* (pp. 177-198). Beverly Hills, CA: Sage.

Baker, S. & Sadd, S. (1979). *Court employment project final report.* New York: Vera Institute.

Bem, D.J. & Honorton, C. (1994). Does psi exist? Replicable evidence for an anomalous process of information transfer. *Psychological Bulletin, 115*, 4-18.

Brannen, S.J. & Rubin, A. (1996). Comparing the effectiveness of gender-specific and couples groups in a court-mandated spouse abuse treatment program. *Research on Social Work Practice, 6*, 405-424.

Buzawa, E., & Buzawa, C. (1996). *Domestic violence: The criminal justice response* (2nd edition). Newbury Park: Sage Publications.

Chen, H., Bersani, C., Myers, S.C., & Denton, R. (1989). Evaluating the effectiveness of a court sponsored abuser treatment program. *Journal of Family Violence, 4*, 309-322.

Cohen, J. (1992). Statistical power analysis. *Current Directions in Psychological Science, 1*, 98-101.

Cohen, J. (1988). *Statistical power analysis for the behavioral sciences* (2nd ed.). Hillsdale, NJ: Lawrence Erlbaum Associates, Inc.

Crowell, N., & Burgess, A.W. (Eds.). (1996). *Understanding violence against women*. Washington, DC: National Academy Press.

Davis, R.C., Smith, B.E. & Nickles, L. (1997). *Prosecuting domestic violence cases with reluctant victims: Assessing two novel approaches*. Washington, D.C.: American Bar Association.

Davis, R.C. & Taylor, B.G. (1997a). *A Randomized Experiment of the Effects of Batterers' Treatment: Summary of Preliminary Research Findings*. Paper presented at the 5th Intnl. Family Violence Research Conference, Durham, NH.

Davis, R.C. & Taylor, B.G. (1997b). A proactive response to family violence: The results of a randomized experiment. *Criminology, 35*(2), 307-333.

Dobash, R.P., Dobash, R.E., Cavanagh, K., & Lewis, R. (1995). Evaluating criminal justice programmes for violent men. In R.E. Dobash, R.P. Dobash & L. Noaks (Eds.), *Gender and crime*. Cardiff, Wales: University of Wales Press.

Dobash, R., Dobash, R.E., Cavanagh, K., & Lewis, R. (1996). Re-education programmes for violent men–an evaluation. *Research Findings, 46*, 1-4.

Dunford, F.W. (1997). *History of the San Diego project and baseline data, the San Diego Navy Project*. Working draft, University of Colorado.

Dutton, D.G. (1986). The outcome of court-mandated treatment for wife assault: A quasi-experimental evaluation. *Violence and Victims, 1*(3), 163-175.

Dutton, D.G. (1988). *The domestic assault of women: Psychological and criminal justice perspectives*. Boston, MA: Allyn & Bacon.

Dutton, D.G. (1995). *The domestic assault of women: Psychological and criminal justice perspectives* (rev. ed.). Vancouver: UBC Press.

Edleson, J.L., & Syers, M. (1990). Relative effectiveness of group treatments for men who batter. *Social Work Research and Abstracts, 26* (2), 10-17.

Eisikovits, Z.C. & Edelson, J.L. (1989). Intervening with men who batter: A critical review of the literature. *Social Service Review, 37*, 384-414.

Ewing, W., Lindsey, M., & Pomerantz, J. (1984). *Battering: An AMMEND manual for helpers*. Denver, CO: AMMEND.

Fagan, J. (1996). The criminalization of domestic violence: Promises and limits. *NIJ Research Report* (January). Washington, DC: National Institute of Justice, U.S. Department of Justice.

Fagan, J., Friedman, E., Wexler, S. & Lewis, V.L. (1984). *National Family Violence Evaluation: Final Report. Volume 1: Executive summary and Analytic Findings.* San Francisco: URSA Institute.

Feazell, C.S., Mayers, R.S., & Deschner, J. (1984). Services for men who batter: Implications for programs and policies. *Family Relations, 33*, 217-223.

Feder, L. (1996). A test of the efficacy of court-mandated counseling for domestic violence offenders: A Broward County experiment. Proposal submitted to the National Institute of Justice. Florida Atlantic University, Boca Raton, Florida.

Ganley, A. (1987). Perpetrators of domestic violence: An overview of counseling the court-mandated client. In D.J. Sonkin (Ed.), *Domestic violence on trial: Psychological and legal dimensions of family violence* (pp. 155-173). New York: Springer.

Garner, J., Fagan, J., & Maxwell, C. (1995). Published findings from the spouse assault replication program: A critical review. *Journal of Quantitative Criminology, 11*, 3-28.

Gartin, P.R. (1995). Dealing with design failures in randomized field experiments: Analytic issues regarding the evaluation of treatment effects. *Journal of Research in Crime and Delinquency, 32*, 425-445.

Goldkamp, J.S. (1996). *The role of drug and alcohol abuse in domestic violence and its treatment: Dade county's domestic violence court experiment* (Final Report). Philadelphia, PA: Crime and Justice Research Institute.

Gondolf, E. (1997a). *Multi-site evaluation of batterer intervention systems: A summary of preliminary findings.* Indiana, PA: Mid-Atlantic Addiction Training Institute.

Gondolf, E. (1995). *Batterer intervention: What we know and need to know.* Paper presented at the National of Institute of Justice Violence Against Women Strategic Planning Meeting, Washington, DC.

Gondolf, E. (1991). A victim-based assessment of court-mandated counseling for batterers. *Criminal Justice Review, 16* (2), 214-226.

Grusz<nski, R.J., & Carillo, T.P. (1988). Who completes batterer's treatment groups? An empirical investigation. *Journal of Family Violence, 3*, 141-150.

Hamberger, L.K., & Hastings, J.E. (1988). Skills training for treatment of spouse abusers: An outcome study. *Journal of Family Violence, 3*, 121-130.

Hamberger, L.K,. & Hastings, J.E. (1989). Counseling male spouse abusers: Characteristics of treatment completers and dropouts. *Violence and Victims, 4*, 275-286.

Hamberger, L.K., & Hastings, J.E. (1990). Recidivism following spouse abuse abatement counseling: Treatment and program implications. *Violence and Victims, 5*, 157-170.

Hamberger, L.K., & Hastings, J.E. (1993). Court-mandated treatment of men who assault their partners: Issues, controversies, and outcomes. In N.Z. Hilton (Ed.), *Legal responses to wife assault: Current trends and evaluation.* Newbury Park, CA: Sage.

Hanna, C. (1996). No right to choose: Mandated victim participation in domestic violence prosecutions. *Harvard Law Review, 109*(8), 1849-1910.

Harrell, A. (1991). *Evaluation of court-ordered treatment for domestic violence offenders.* Final report to the State Justice Institute. Washington, DC: The Urban Institute.

Harrell, A.V., Roehl, J.A., & Kapsak, K.A. (1988). *Family violence intervention demonstration programs evaluation, volume II: Case studies*. Report submitted to the Bureau of Justice Assistance. Washington, DC: The Institute of Social Analysis.

Harris, R., Savage, S., Jones, T., & Brooke, W. (1988). A comparison of treatments for abusive men and their partners within a family-service agency. *Canadian Journal of Community Mental Health, 7*(2), 147-155.

Healey, K., Smith, C., & O'Sullivan, C. (1997). *Batterer intervention: Program approaches and criminal justice strategies*. Report of Abt Associates to the National Institute of Justice, Washington, DC.

Maiuro, R.D., Cahn, T.S., Vitaliano, P.P. & Zegree, J.B. (1987, August) *Treatment for domestically violent men: Outcome and follow-up data*. Paper presented at the meeting of the American Psychological Association, New York.

Martin, S., Sechrest, L., & Redner, R. (Eds.) (1981). *New directions in the rehabilitation of criminal offenders*. Washington, D.C.: National Academy of Sciences Press.

Palmer, S.E., Brown, R.A., & Barrera, M.E. (1992). Group treatment program for abusive husbands: Long-term evaluation. *American Journal of Orthopsychiatry, 62*(2), 276-283.

Rebovich, D.J. (1996). Prosecution response to domestic violence: Results of a survey of large jurisdictions. In E.S. Buzawa & C.G. Buzawa (Eds.), *Do arrests and restraining orders work?* Thousand Oaks, CA: Sage.

Rosenbaum, A., & O'Leary, K. (1986). The treatment of marital violence. In N.S. Jacobsen & A.S. Gurman (Eds.), *Clinical handbook of marital therapy*. NY: Guilford.

Rosenfeld, B.D. (1992). Court-ordered treatment of spouse abuse. *Clinical Psychology Review, 12*, 205-226.

Rosenthal, R. (1991). *Meta-analytic procedures for social research* (2nd ed.). Newbury Park, CA: Sage.

Saunders, D.G. (1996a). Interventions for men who batter: Do we know what works. *Psychotherapy in Practice, 2*(3), 81-93.

Saunders, D.G. (1996b). Feminist-cognitive-behavioral and process-psychodynamic treatments for men who batter: Interaction of abuser traits and treatment models.*Violence and Victims, 11*(1), 37-50.

Saunders, D.G., & Azar, S. (1989). Family violence treatment programs: Descriptions and evaluation. In L. Ohlin & M. Tonry (Eds.), *Family violence: Crime and justice, a review of research* (pp. 481-546). Chicago, IL: University of Chicago Press.

Sherman, L.W. (1992b). *Policing domestic violence: Experiments and dilemmas*. New York: Free Press.

Sullivan, C.M., Rumptz, M.H., Campbell, R., Eby, K.K., & Davidson, W.S. (1996). Retaining participants in longitudinal community research: A comprehensive protocol. *Journal of Applied Behavioral Science, 32*(3), 262-276.

Taylor, B. (1995). An evaluation of the domestic violence prevention project. Internal report. Research Division, Victim Services, New York.

Tolman, R.M., & Bennett, L.W. (1990). Quantitative research on men who batter. *Journal of Interpersonal Violence, 5* (1), 87-118.

Tolman, R.M. & Edelson, J.L. (1995). Interventions for men who batter: A review of research. In S.M. Stith & M.A. Straus (Eds.), *Understanding partner violence: Prevalence, causes, consequences, and solutions.* Minneapolis, MN: National Council on Family Relations.

Utts, J. (1991). Replication and meta-analysis in parapsychology. *Statistical Science, 6,* 363-378.

Weinstein, G.S. & Levin, B.L. (1989). Effect of crossover on the statistical power of randomized studies. *Annals of Thoracic Surgery, 48,* 490-95.

Index

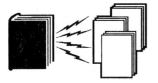

Haworth
DOCUMENT DELIVERY
SERVICE

This valuable service provides a single-article order form for any article from a Haworth journal.

- *Time Saving:* No running around from library to library to find a specific article.
- *Cost Effective:* All costs are kept down to a minimum.
- *Fast Delivery:* Choose from several options, including same-day FAX.
- *No Copyright Hassles:* You will be supplied by the original publisher.
- *Easy Payment:* Choose from several easy payment methods.

Open Accounts Welcome for ...
- Library Interlibrary Loan Departments
- Library Network/Consortia Wishing to Provide Single-Article Services
- Indexing/Abstracting Services with Single Article Provision Services
- Document Provision Brokers and Freelance Information Service Providers

---

MAIL or *FAX* THIS ENTIRE ORDER FORM TO:

Haworth Document Delivery Service
The Haworth Press, Inc.
10 Alice Street
Binghamton, NY 13904-1580

or FAX: 1-800-895-0582
or CALL: 1-800-429-6784
9am-5pm EST

PLEASE SEND ME PHOTOCOPIES OF THE FOLLOWING SINGLE ARTICLES:

1) Journal Title: _____

   Vol/Issue/Year:_____Starting & Ending Pages:_____

   Article Title:_____

   _____

2) Journal Title: _____

   Vol/Issue/Year:_____Starting & Ending Pages:_____

   Article Title:_____

   _____

3) Journal Title: _____

   Vol/Issue/Year:_____Starting & Ending Pages:_____

   Article Title:_____

   _____

4) Journal Title: _____

   Vol/Issue/Year:_____Starting & Ending Pages:_____

   Article Title:_____

   _____

(See other side for Costs and Payment Information)

COSTS: Please figure your cost to order quality copies of an article.

1. Set-up charge per article: $8.00
   ($8.00 × number of separate articles) _____

2. Photocopying charge for each article:

   1-10 pages: $1.00 _____

   11-19 pages: $3.00 _____

   20-29 pages: $5.00 _____

   30+ pages: $2.00/10 pages _____

3. Flexicover (optional): $2.00/article _____

4. Postage & Handling: US: $1.00 for the first article/

   $.50 each additional article _____

   Federal Express: $25.00 _____

   Outside US: $2.00 for first article/

   $.50 each additional article _____

5. Same-day FAX service: $.50 per page _____

GRAND TOTAL: _____

METHOD OF PAYMENT: (please check one)

❏ Check enclosed   ❏ Please ship and bill. PO # _____
(sorry we can ship and bill to bookstores only! All others must pre-pay)

❏ Charge to my credit card: ❏ Visa; ❏ MasterCard; ❏ Discover;
❏ American Express;

Account Number: _____ Expiration date: _____

Signature: **X** _____

Name: _____ Institution: _____

Address: _____

_____

City: _____ State: _____ Zip: _____

Phone Number: _____ FAX Number: _____

MAIL or *FAX* THIS ENTIRE ORDER FORM TO:

Haworth Document Delivery Service
The Haworth Press, Inc.
10 Alice Street
Binghamton, NY 13904-1580

or FAX: 1-800-895-0582
or CALL: 1-800-429-6784
(9am-5pm EST)

HIDDEN ADDICTIONS

A Pastoral Response to the Abuse of Legal Drugs

Bridget Clare McKeever, PhD, SSL
Director of Diocesan Spirituality Center,
Diocese of Salt Lake City, Utah

"Reveals the critical role that a male-oriented society plays, particularly in the lives of women. . . . The creative and insightful suggestions for a pastoral response make this a valuable aid for both clergy and lay counselors alike."
Rev. Dr. David W. Randle; President and CEO, UCC Wellness, Health, and Lifestyle Education Center, Sandy, Utah

The only book of its kind, **Hidden Addictions** is a concise, readable pastoral perspective on the creeping epidemic of legal drug abuse. Its illuminating case vignettes show you the social roots of addiction and give you the spiritual and religious resources necessary to put you and your loved ones on the road to holistic recovery.

So whether you're a pastor whose congregation is suffering, a social worker administering to addicted clientele, or a campus minister, this book will give you the pragmatism and awareness you need to heal the wounded soul.

Contents

Foreword • Preface • Acknowledgments

$29.95 hard. ISBN: 0-7890-0266-3.
(Outside US/Canada/Mexico: $36.00)
$14.95 soft. ISBN: 0-7890-0267-1.
(Outside US/Canada/Mexico: $18.00)
1998. 96 pp. with Index.
Features case studies and a bibliography.

Please complete the information below or tape your business card in this area.

☐ YES, please send me **Hidden Addictions**
— in hard at $29.95 ISBN: 0-7890-0266-3. (Outside US/Canada/Mexico: $36.00)
— in soft at $14.95 ISBN: 0-7890-0267-1. (Outside US/Canada/Mexico: $18.00)

- Individual orders outside US, Canada, and Mexico must be
  prepaid by check or credit card.
- Discounts are not available on 5+ text prices and not available in conjunction
  with any other discount.
- Discount not applicable on books priced under $15.00.
- 5+ text prices are not available for jobbers and wholesalers.
- Postage & handling: in US: $4.00 for first book; $1.50 for each additional book.
  Outside US: $5.00 for first book; $2.00 for each additional book.
- NY, MN, and OH residents: please add appropriate sales tax.
- Canadian residents: please add 7% GST after postage & handling.
- Payment in UNESCO coupons welcome.
- If paying in Canadian dollars, use current exchange rate to convert to US dollars.
- Please allow 3-4 weeks for delivery after publication.
- Prices and discounts subject to change without notice.

Signature _____

☐ **BILL ME LATER($5 service charge will be added).**
(Not available for individuals outside US/Canada/Mexico. Service charge is
waived for/jobbers/wholesalers/booksellers.)
☐ Check here if billing address is different from shipping address and attach purchase
order and billing address information.

☐ **PAYMENT ENCLOSED $**_____
(Payment must be in US or Canadian dollars by check or money order drawn on a US or Canadian bank.)

☐ **PLEASE BILL MY CREDIT CARD:**
☐ AmEx ☐ Diners Club ☐ Discover ☐ Eurocard ☐ Master Card ☐ Visa

Account Number _____

Expiration Date _____

Signature _____
May we open a confidential credit card account for you for possible future purchases? ( ) Yes ( ) No

THE HAWORTH PRESS, INC., 10 Alice Street, Binghamton, NY 13904-1580 USA

FAX

NAME _____

INSTITUTION _____

ADDRESS _____

CITY _____

STATE _____ ZIP _____

COUNTRY _____

COUNTY (NY residents only) _____

TEL _____

E-MAIL _____

May we use your e-mail address for confirmations and other types of information?
( ) Yes ( ) No. We appreciate receiving your e-mail address and fax number. Haworth would like
to e-mail or fax special discount offers to you, as a preferred customer. We will never **share, rent, or
exchange** your e-mail address or fax number. We regard such actions as an invasion of your privacy.

☐ YES, please send me **Hidden Addictions** (ISBN: 0-7890-0267-1) to consider on a 60-day
examination basis. I understand that I will receive an invoice payable within 60 days, or that
if I decide to adopt the book, my invoice will be cancelled. I understand that I will be
billed at the lowest price. (Offer available only to teaching faculty in US, Canada, and
Mexico.)

Signature _____

Course Title(s) _____

Current Text(s) _____

Enrollment _____

Semester _____

Office Tel _____ Decision Date _____

Hours _____

(20) (15) 10/99 BIC99

FAX